ORGANISATIONAL STRUCTURE
An Essential Lever in Managing Change

Patrick Cunneen

BLACKHALL
Publishing

This book was typeset by Paragon Press, Inc. for

Blackhall Publishing
33 Carysfort Avenue
Blackrock
Co. Dublin
Ireland

e-mail: info@blackhallpublishing.com
www.blackhallpublishing.com

ISBN: 978-1-84218-154-6

A catalogue record for this book is available from the British Library.

Printed in Ireland by ColourBooks Ltd.

To my parents, Bill and Nancy Cunneen.

ABOUT THE AUTHOR

Patrick Cunneen has over three decades of experience as a practising manager, consultant and teacher, across three continents.

Pat is currently on assignment as executive vice president of human resources at Abu Dhabi Aircraft Technologies in the United Arab Emirates (UAE). For over a decade, he was director of human resources for global manufacturing at Analog Devices Inc., a US-based high-technology semiconductor manufacturer. In that role, he had HR responsibility for plants in Massachusetts, California, Ireland, the Philippines and Taiwan. He has worked and lived in Ireland, the US and the UAE.

Pat is also currently adjunct professor of HR management at the University of Limerick in Ireland, where he contributed to strategic HRM on UL's corporate MBA and other executive education programmes. He is a founder and director of Lighthouse Organisational Consultants Ltd., a consulting firm specialising in organisational development, HR consulting, organisational change and executive coaching.

Pat is a fellow of the Chartered Institute of Personnel and Development (CIPD). He has presented at and chaired conferences in Ireland, the US, the UK, Turkey and the Philippines.

PREFACE

Continuous change in the business environment and competitive land-scape is the norm today. The agility of firms in responding to change, through reorganising and restructuring themselves to meet these challenges and opportunities, can be a source of significant competitive advantage.

The rationale for this book is to explore and consider the significance of organisation structural design in helping organisations adapt to the ever-changing business environment.

This book is primarily written for MBA students studying strategy and strategic human resource management (HRM), students of HRM studying for advanced degrees and students of other executive education programmes. However, while the audience is primarily an advanced student population, the book is written in such a way as to be also helpful to business leaders, senior organisational and HR practitioners, and organisational change consultants.

As a HR practitioner, I believe the book should be of particular assistance to senior HR practitioners. Leading business leaders and commentators are looking to the HR function to be a strategic partner in the business. One way for HR to provide strategic support to the business is the capacity to both diagnose organisational structural issues and provide guidance in organisation design for enhanced organisational effectiveness.

ACKNOWLEDGEMENTS

I have had unstinting encouragement and support from my family, friends and colleagues throughout the development and writing of this book.

Thanks to my colleagues at University of Limerick, in particular Dr Sarah Moore and Professor Patrick Flood (now based in Dublin City University) for encouraging to me to write.

Thanks also to my Lighthouse Organisational Consultants colleague Dr Thérèse Brady and to Dr Dave Collings of National University of Ireland, Galway for their continued support, insight and 'shadow editing' throughout the project. I wish to thank good friends and former colleagues, including Eamonn McAvinue and Eamon Ryan, for passionate debate and argument on this and many other topics.

I am grateful to Blackhall Publishing for their faith in the book, and in particular to my editor Elizabeth Brennan for her assistance and guidance throughout the project.

Finally, and most importantly, my heartfelt thanks to those special editors and change-agents of my life – my family. Thanks to Jacinta, Deirdre, Niamh and Eoghan for their ceaseless encouragement and support.

CONTENTS

INTRODUCTION

Up until the 1990s many organisations accepted organisational structure for what it was, however serendipitously it had evolved over time. Managers accepted structure, sometimes feeling powerless when confronted with the prospect of considerable office politics and the challenge of substantial organisational change. Up until this time, many organisational leaders underestimated the power of organisational structure to directly influence and support business strategy. Increasingly, however, many organisations now understand the essential strategic and systemic link between business strategy, structure and other key components, including business processes and people.

There is a conventional wisdom that structure follows strategy (Chandler 1962). However, while university libraries are rich on the topic of business strategy, the topic of organisational structure is not represented nearly so well. Drawing an analogy from architecture and industrial design, where form follows function, organisation design (structure) must follow function (strategy). As with architecture, this book seeks to address not only the fundamentals of organisation design but also the relationship of the organisation to its environment.

Continuous change in the business environment and competitive landscape is the norm today. The deftness of a firm's response to those changes through how it reorganises itself to meet challenges and opportunities is a source of significant competitive advantage. Leading organisations centralise their global supply chain to optimise manufacturing and supply chain processes across business units, in order to achieve economies of scale to lower costs and improve cycle times. Global service providers such as actuarial firms and IT support are being restructured to provide global clients with a timely and consistent service around the world.

My approach to this work reflects my experience of over three decades in business, across three continents. Hopefully, it is sufficiently balanced with management theory and practice to make it useful to students of management and practitioners alike. I have sought to bring together the essence of the work presented in management theory and organisational behaviour and the ever-evolving contemporary approaches to organisation design by some leading firms and commentators.

The book was developed because I believe that organisational structural design is not sufficiently addressed in many business schools. It continues to surprise me that so many managers are not particularly conscious of such basic concepts as hierarchical levels and spans of control or understand the essential nature of matrix structures. I believe that it is important for managers to understand not only the essentials of organisation design but, as importantly, to understand its capacity to influence and support strategic organisational change.

Chapter 1 describes the essential link between strategy and structure. Chapters 2 and 3 explain the basic principles of organisation design and the different functional, product and geographic structures. Chapters 4, 5 and 6 will review more contemporary concepts such as matrix management, team-based structures, 'virtual organisations', 'front-back' and other hybrid structures. Chapter 7 considers organisation design issues in the integration of mergers and acquisitions. Chapter 8 explores the management of organisational change, and discusses models and essentials for successful change. The final chapter outlines a change management process for organisational restructuring.

I use real-world examples from such industry leaders as Procter & Gamble, Cisco and Hewlett Packard to illustrate and support points of theory. Drawing on my own experience, I have developed and presented case studies that demonstrate the application of the principles to authentic situations for critical analysis and debate.

CHAPTER 1

THE ESSENTIAL CONNECTION BETWEEN STRATEGY AND STRUCTURE

Introduction

This chapter focuses on the essential relationship between strategy and structure. It considers the conventional wisdom that structure follows strategy and the sequencing possibilities between strategy and structure. The chapter examines the influence of the business on structure and the need for organisations to be sufficiently agile and able to adapt to emergent strategy. Finally, it acknowledges that, while the focus of the book is on organisational structure, other elements of organisation, such as organisational processes and people, must also be taken into account.

Structure Follows Strategy?

Chandler (1962) first highlighted the importance of the connection between strategy and organisational structure. In his work *Strategy and Structure,* much of which was based on the experience of General Motors under Alfred Sloan, Chandler highlighted that different strategies call for different organisational structures; that long-term strategies should be the dominant factor in deciding organisational structure. Chandler's view, which gave rise to the well-known idea that structure follows strategy, is supported by Miles and Snow (1986), who stress that business strategies must be congruent with the external environment and that each of these strategies requires different structures. They offer the view that entrepreneurial, 'first-to-market' prospectors require flexible, decentralised, organic structures; and strategies that offer stable, cost competitive products (defenders) require a more mechanistic, functional structure with centralised decision making and control.

3

Porter's (1980) framework describing low-cost and differentiated strategies further reinforces the need for congruence between strategy and structure. Porter points out that low-cost strategies need a substantial efficiency-oriented structure, including strong central authority and control, and highly efficient process management. Conversely, a differentiated strategy requires a flexible, loosely-knit structure with good horizontal coordination and with a strong emphasis on brand management and new product development.

Keats and Hitt (1988) offer a counterpoint to Chandler's proposition that structure follows strategy, suggesting that the causal relationship may be in the opposite direction. They suggest that the choice of a structure leads to a pattern of decision making, which favours the continuance of that structure. They suggest that structures, once chosen, exhibit inertial properties. There is no doubt that, due to office politics and/or a lack of capability in managing organisational change effectively, many organisations display some inertia in changing structure to address a changing strategy. Mintzberg (1990) uses the analogy of footsteps to explain his view of what he terms the reciprocal nature of strategy and structure. On one step, the right foot leads the left but on the next step, the left leads the right. In his analogy, Mintzberg suggests that strategy leads structure but then, in turn, structure leads or influences strategy. Whichever way the causal relationship flows between strategy and structure, however, Chandler, Keats and Hitt, and Mintzberg all agree that there is an important connection between strategy and structure.

The Nature of the Business and Structure

The context of the business environment naturally has a significant influence on the structural design of the organisation. One such environmental dimension is the operational complexity of the firm.

Organisations, such as supermarkets or fast-food restaurant chains, which have low complexity and are basically homogeneous, can operate with a relatively simple structure. In Ireland, the Superquinn supermarket chain was structured fundamentally by store, with the corporate office set up as a support activity to the individual stores.

Businesses that have a much higher degree of organisational complexity, such as semiconductor, software development and biotechnology companies, require a more complex structure to manage their businesses. A semiconductor firm might have its product designed in Santa Clara, its software developed in India, and have the product manufactured in Taiwan by a third-party contract manufacturer. In such organisations, individual departments have much higher levels of interdependency and need greater levels of coordination and control.

Another dimension of the business environment that has an influence on organisational structure is the degree of stability prevalent in the business. A business that is relatively stable holds few surprises; and the manager's job is to ensure that employees follow tried and trusted procedures. Organisations in businesses that are less stable and more dynamic, continuously present uncertainties and greater managerial challenges. It follows that such organisations require greater managerial competence and sophistication, e.g. biotechnology.

These differing business environments significantly impact on such structural design choices as hierarchical layers and spans of control, which are discussed in Chapter 2.

Organisational Structure Design Needs to be Dynamic

It is very important that whatever structure is selected, it is regularly reviewed for continued relevance to the business strategy and the changing business environment. As strategies change to respond to changes in technology, deregulation and customer demands, so too the organisational structure needs to evolve to support and remain in sync with those strategic changes. Pettigrew stresses the verb 'organising' over the noun 'organisation', suggesting that the process of continuous review needs to be active, not passive: 'few firms see organisational change as moving from one static structure to another' (1999: 523).

Mintzberg (1985) distinguishes between intended strategy (deliberate) and evolved strategy (emergent). Emergent strategy refers to the decisions that emerge from organisations adapting to changing circumstances and the ways in which the intended strategy is adapted and evolved.

5

Theory & Practice

During the 1980s, a large, well-known US semiconductor company was structured by manufacturing technology. Each division, which operated quite autonomously at the time, had its own particular wafer fabrication process technology. Through this difference in process technology, one division's products were very fast but required more power while another division's products required less power but weren't quite as fast. So customers, who were original equipment manufacturers, would buy from one or other of the divisions, depending on the needs of their application. However, as the decade of the 1980s wore on, the technologists in both divisions had improved their respective processes to such an extent that they were able to produce new products, with both high-speed and low-power consumption features. As these newer products evolved and with the high degree of divisional autonomy, marketing managers in both divisions began to compete with each other for the same business opportunities; marketing managers were 'trampling' their customers. Only after several years did the organisation truly realise the extent of the situation and reorganised by market sector, e.g. automotive, telecommunications, and so on.

This is a clear example of what Mintzberg describes as emergent strategy. It is so important to regularly review the relevance of organisational structure in the light of a continuously changing business environment and consequent strategies.

There is more than just Strategy and Structure

Peters and Waterman (1982), and their colleagues at McKinsey's Organizational Effectiveness Practice in San Francisco, emphatically reinforced the need for connection between strategy and structure but added that other important elements of the organisational jigsaw needed equal consideration. In addition to strategy and structure, they added systems, style, skill, staff and something they called 'superordinate' goals (higher order values and aspirations). Their alliteration was deliberate and their model became universally known as the McKinsey '7S Model' for organisational effectiveness. Their assertion is that productive organisational change is not simply a matter of structure but that effective organisational change is really a close-knit relationship between structure, strategy, systems, style, skills, staff and 'superordinate' goals.

Galbraith (2002) supports this wider, more comprehensive focus with his 'star model'. In his model, Galbraith tightens the number of jigsaw pieces to five elements: strategy, structure, processes, people and rewards. Galbraith warns that most design efforts invest far too much time drawing the organisational charts and far too little time on processes, people and rewards. Figure 1.1 shows the essential elements or critical jigsaw pieces for effective organisational planning. It shows not only the internally focused elements but also reflects the winds of the external environment, which constantly buffet every organisation.

Figure 1.1: Key Elements in Organisational Architecture

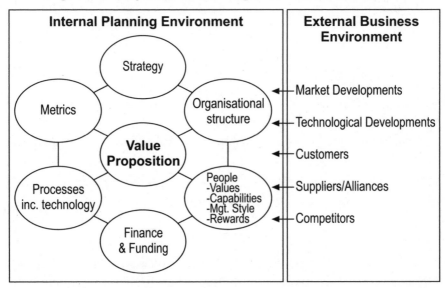

While wholeheartedly supportive of the widest architectural focus for productive organisational change advocated by Peters *et al.* and Galbraith, the particular focal point of this book is to explore and discuss the element of structure.

Chapter 2

Fundamentals of Organisation Design

Having considered the essential relationship between strategy and structure in Chapter 1, this chapter steps back a little and examines some of the basic concepts of organisation design, including a brief discussion on bureaucracy and post-bureaucracy. It examines the fundamentals of organisational structure design such as organisational charts, hierarchical layers and spans of control, staff and line relationships, and explores the centralisation/decentralisation continuum.

Bureaucracy

Up until the industrial revolution, most industry, such as it was, was very small-scale and was primarily characterised by master-servant relationships.

Max Weber, a German sociologist and philosopher, advanced the concept of bureaucracy as an effective means of managing a business. Based on the German word *bureau*, meaning office, Weber (1947) proposed a set of principles about how best to manage an office or business. His proposition included clear lines of authority and hierarchy, operating policies and procedures, and clear job descriptions with authority commensurate with responsibility and record-keeping. Interestingly, many of these basic principles are still very much in evidence in organisations today.

Weber introduced basic rational principles of management into an era of the post-industrial revolution which was characterised by a lack of structure, efficiency and record-keeping. It is hardly surprising that Weber's concepts were quickly and almost universally adopted.

The benefits of Weber's bureaucracy were to be found in detailed procedures, leading to conformity and adherence to defined standards. This mechanistic system included the following principles:

- The organisation operates to a defined set of rules and procedures intended to control employee behaviour.
- Employees must apply clear and impersonal rules and procedures in making decisions; there is no room for discretion.
- Each employee's job has a clearly defined description and set of expectations.
- Each layer of the hierarchy is under the direct supervision and control of the person above them in the hierarchy.
- Employees are selected on the basis of their abilities and qualifications.
- Promotion is by seniority or ability, depending on the judgement of their supervisors.

Weber, through his interest in power and authority, advanced the concept of legitimate authority or position power. Legitimate authority is where we accept orders, instructions or requests from supervisors not because of their family position, class or caste but because their role is legitimate in the context of the organisation's goals; because the supervisor's orders seem reasonable and rational in pursuit of the goals of the organisation. As a manager, I can reasonably request my subordinate to prepare a monthly sales report but not to do my weekend grocery shopping (Grey 2005).

Weber believed that an organisation based on legitimate authority would be more effective and efficient than one based on charismatic authority, because the continuity of authority depended on formal structures rather than on any one individual person who might leave or die (Huczynski and Buchanan 2001).

Coincident with the introduction of Weber's concepts of bureaucracy, Frederick Winslow Taylor's *Principles of Scientific Management* (1911) introduced scientific work measurement and work design, which sought to increase operator productive output though the reduction in variation of work methods, seeking efficiency, predictability and control. Taylor's principles of scientific management included:

- A clear delineation and division of tasks between managers and workers; between the 'thinkers and the doers'.
- Scientific measurement to establish the best way to carry out a task.
- Careful selection of people most suited to carry out the task.
- Careful training of the person selected to carry out the task in the specified manner.
- Surveillance of the workers through hierarchy and close supervision.

These concepts were by no means confined to the capitalist economies of the West. Lenin and Stalin used the concepts to speed up the industrialisation of the largely agrarian economy of the Soviet Union (Merkle 1980). Taylor's scientific management was a powerful and successful attempt to understand production efforts and at the same time to ensure that it was management who controlled output, not the workers. In seeking to maximise predictability of output, scientific management had the effect of removing, and even outlawing, workers' discretion and sending out the message that workers were no more than operational cogs in the organisational machine. This system of management was wonderfully lampooned in the Charlie Chaplin film *Modern Times*.

Today, while some of these basic principles of bureaucracy are still very much in evidence in organisations, the term bureaucracy itself carries a certain negative connotation, often pejoratively referred to as 'red tape'. It is often associated with such terms as rigidity, inefficiency, and slow-moving and ridiculous procedures. Ironically, while Weber introduced bureaucracy as a means to improving efficiency, today it is more often associated with inefficiency. There is indeed the paradox that trade unions sometimes resort to a 'work to rule' in pursuit of an industrial relations claim. Implicit in this action is that union members will only do exactly what is defined in their job descriptions and nothing more.

The combination of Weber's bureaucracy and Taylor's scientific management hugely complemented each other. The combined and complementary concepts remained in vogue through generations of managers, through almost three-quarters of the twentieth century.

Post-Bureaucracy

Western economies in the 1970s and early 1980s were moving from the mass production of standard products to shorter production cycles for more differentiated markets. In addition, the slowing down of productivity growth and the significant increase in the competitive and quality challenges from Japan were leading Western firms to the conclusion that bureaucracy and Taylorist methods, which had served them so well in the past, had perhaps outlived some of their usefulness and were now limiting growth. These shifts called for much greater organisational flexibility and change and led to the search for new forms of organisation that would be more conducive to higher productivity, quality and all-round innovation (Child 2005). Hecksher (1994) describes a post-bureaucratic organisational type as follows:

- Rules and policies are replaced with consensus and dialogue, which are based on capacity to influence rather than hierarchy and status.
- Responsibilities are assigned on the basis of competence rather than hierarchy.
- Employment type is much more flexible and varied, with full- and part-time employees, contract workers and consultants.

Post-bureaucracy (also referred to as 'post-industrial' and 'post-Fordism') refers to a variety of newer approaches to markets, customers and employees in the emerging global marketplace. These include flexible production systems, flatter structures, and the application of human relations management theories, including the multi-skilling of workers. Such changes have given rise to post-bureaucracy terminology such as the 'virtual' and 'networked' organisations, many of which are explored in later chapters.

The shift towards post-bureaucratic forms was neither universally nor immediately adopted and the polarities presented in Table 2.1 should really be seen as polarities on a continuum. Organisations are rarely completely bureaucratic or post-bureaucratic. As a generalisation, larger organisations, especially government departments, tend to exhibit higher levels of bureaucracy than smaller, customer-focused organisations.

Table 2.1: Evolution to Post-Bureaucracy

Bureaucracy	Post-Bureaucracy
Protected national markets	Globalisation
Mass production	Flexible production including outsourcing
Manufacturing is king	The customer is king
Rules and procedures	Dialogue and consensus
Work as an individual	Team-based work
Taylorism and work measurement	Human relations theories of management
Hierarchy rules	Competence rules

> ### Theory & Practice
> *Copying much of General Motors' original bureaucratic structures, the Ford Motor Company is a good example of an organisation that had a very rigid hierarchical structure and motorised assembly lines, with assembly workers reduced to doing narrowly scoped, highly repetitive tasks and where every action was defined explicitly in a policies and procedures manual. However, the Japanese auto industry made such inroads into the US markets during the 1980s that Ford was forced to jettison their traditional bureaucracy, which was considered too slow and inflexible for such a dynamic marketplace and they began to place a much greater focus on product quality and employee involvement. As a response to the Japanese competition, Ford began to promote greater individual and team discretion, and creativity. They created less rigid team-based structures that would facilitate greater empowerment and were focused on product innovation and quality.*

If there was just one word to explain the move away from many of the elements of bureaucracy and scientific management in business, it would be globalisation. Increased competition, not just on price but also on product and service quality has either transformed or terminated organisations. Deregulation and international agreements to liberalise trade and open up markets, together with high-speed communications technology, has fundamentally changed how companies are structured and managed. Globalisation has led to the search for new forms of organisational structure. Such structures are explored and discussed in later chapters.

Organisational Charts

Organisational charts are intended to depict the formal reporting relationships or 'chain of command' within an organisation. This schematic, or 'wiring diagram', portrays how work is coordinated, and illustrates both the number of layers in the structure and the span of control of managers and supervisors at each layer or level.

Typically, the organisational chart resembles a pyramid, or an inverted tree (see Figure 2.1). With its origins in earliest military structures, this chain of command flows in straight, unbroken vertical lines from the chief executive to the most junior participant in the organisation.

The organisational chart is usually the first thing handed to anyone inquiring about structure. Mintzberg (1979) and Nadler *et al.* (1992) warn that, while most organisations continue to find organisational charts indispensable, many organisational theorists reject them, believing that they are an inadequate description of what really takes place inside an organisation. Mintzberg acknowledges that, while the organisational chart does not reflect the full complexity of an organisational structure or its informal relationships, it does represent an accurate picture of the division of labour 'showing at a glance (a) what positions exist in the organisation, (b) how these are grouped into units, and (c) how formal authority flows among them' (1979: 37).

Hellriegel *et al.* (1998) state that clarity of reporting direction is at the core of the chain of command and they emphasise unity of command, which holds that no subordinate should receive orders from more than one supervisor. They stress that without unity of command, instructions will be both cloudy and confusing. While accepting the broad principles of unity of command as essentially sound, the complexity in organisations today often involves multiple sources of instructions and direction. We will return to this topic later in subsequent chapters when we discuss team-based structures and matrix management.

Organisational Layers

Examining the somewhat simplistic organisational chart shown in Figure 2.1 will help identify and clarify some of the most basic concepts of organisational structure, namely organisational layers and spans of control. Organisational layers or hierarchy refers to the number of management/supervisory levels or layers in the firm. To determine the number of organisational layers, count the levels or links in the chain of command from the top to the bottom of the longest chain in the organisation. An organisation with relatively few layers is generally described as a flat structure and an organisation with many layers is described as a tall structure.

Figure 2.1: Organisational Structure – Chain of Command

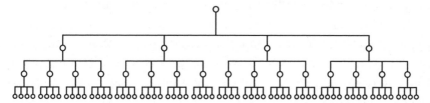

Not surprisingly, organisation size is typically the biggest influence on the number of layers in the structure of the organisation. Your local 7–11 convenience store is likely to have only two layers. The store owner is one layer and the sales assistants represent the second layer. On the other hand, a large international bank is likely to have upwards of eight or more layers. The Roman Catholic Church is an interesting example of a flat structure. The Church, with almost a billion members, has only four organisational layers: curate, parish priest, bishop and the Pope. While there are other grades, e.g. arch-bishop and cardinal, bishops have a direct reporting relationship to the Pope in Rome. Motorola set up a new telecoms assembly facility in Easter Inch in east Scotland in 1991, employing 2000 people and with a plan to have a maximum structure of four layers from top to bottom, using a team-based structure. This case is detailed in Chapter 5, which explores team-based structures.

The general experience is that in flatter structures, communication up and down the organisation is faster and less distorted; decisions can be made more quickly, which often means that the firm can be faster in responding to customers; and employees at lower levels feel more in touch with senior management. One difficulty in flatter organisations from an employee's career perspective is that there are fewer opportunities for promotion because there are fewer steps up the ladder. Some organisations have addressed this issue by promoting greater mobility across roles and providing more promotable opportunities based on individual contributions. In that regard, some companies explicitly reward lateral career movement in order to promote greater flexibility and broader organisational learning. Such structures encourage continued self-development and acquisition of multiple competencies by employees, and does not pit individuals against one another in competition for a fixed pool of organisational rewards, be they pay increases, bonuses, stock options or promotions (Mohrman *et al.* 1993).

The experience in taller structures, not surprisingly, is the opposite. Communication tends to be slower and more likely to have distortion, and decisions take longer. Management costs are obviously higher because of the greater population of managers required. Throughout the 1990s, due to increased global competition, a great many companies have engaged in extensive middle management de-layering, resulting in the redundancy of thousands of middle managers across the US and elsewhere. One of the first things Greg Dyke did when he became director general of the BBC in 2000 was to flatten the top two layers of that organisation.

Given the disadvantages of tall organisational structures noted above and the extensive de-layering programmes over the past decade and a half, it is hardly surprising that many firms now have strict controls over proposals to create new jobs, which have the potential to create an additional layer either inadvertently or otherwise. These firms take a more strategic, explicitly stated view of their organisational structure. However, it is surprising that so many firms still do not have an awareness of this important strategic design issue and seem to allow their organisational layers to grow 'organically'. The Conference Board (http://www.conference-board.org) reported that managers in a major electronics manufacturing company became much more interested in organisational structures and layers after the publication of an internal benchmarking analysis of organisational structure. After that analysis and some heightened awareness through training, managers simply stopped proposing 'one-over-one' deputy or assistant positions. When considering new positions, which could have the effect of adding an organisational layer, firms need to see a clearly definable and differentiated added value to the new role and layer.

Span of Control

Span of control refers to the number of employees reporting directly to one manager or supervisor. Where there are a large number of employees reporting to a manager, this is described as a broad span of control. Where there are a small number of employees reporting to a manager, this is a narrow span of control.

As one might imagine, there is a direct arithmetic relationship between organisational layers and spans of control. In an organisation of a given size, where the span of control is broad, fewer layers exist between top and bottom. Equally, there are more layers where the span of control is narrow. Contrast two different organisations, one with a tall structure and one with a flat structure, each with a total direct workforce of 4,096 operatives. The tall structure, with a span of control of four, will require a total of 1,365 managers and supervisors to manage the operational community, whereas the flatter structure, with a span of eight, will only require 585 managers and supervisors to manage the same operative population (Robbins 1990).

For over fifty years there was general adherence to the scientific management theorists' 'rule of five'. According to this principle, a manager's span of control should not exceed five. Obviously, this has had the effect of creating a great many tall structures. However, this rule of five was seriously challenged by organisations throughout the 1990s, when layers were greatly reduced and spans of control increased. Today, almost universally, the emphasis is on broadening spans of control in order to flatten organisations. Some industries, including automotive products and electrical goods, have flattened their structures through improved supervisory training, IT enhanced production control systems and well-trained, self-directed work teams. In some cases, at the first level, this has resulted in spans of control of up to 1:100.

There are a number of influences or contextual factors that can have a bearing on spans of control. For example, an experienced manager of a largely homogeneous manufacturing operation, where employees perform relatively simple and repetitive tasks, should be able to manage a much wider span of control than a product marketing manager, who also has to make an individual functional contribution to the business as well as having their managerial responsibilities. In general, influences on span of control include:

- *The nature of the work to be done:* subordinates who handle straightforward and repetitive tasks usually require less supervision allowing for a wider span of control. Conversely, subordinates who handle more complex and less repetitive projects typically require a narrower span of control.
- *The managerial competence of the manager:* experienced managers who effectively delegate authority are able to handle wider spans of control.
- *The extent to which the manager has his/her own individual contributor role to play in addition to the supervision of others:* in many scientific or engineering environments, the leader may be expected to make an individual technical contribution in addition to their supervisory responsibilities. The greater the expectation for their technical contribution, the less time they have to supervise others, and therefore they are more likely to have a narrower span of control.
- *The geographic location of the supervised population (co-located or geographically dispersed):* a supervisor who is co-located beside his/her subordinates is likely to be able to manage a wider span of control than someone whose employees are scattered across different locations and time zones.
- *Self-management:* it is probable that experienced, responsible professionals who prefer to work independently and are self-motivated will enable their managers to have wider spans of control.

Line, Staff and Other Organisational Relationships

Like much of the origins of organisational structure, the concepts of line and staff relationships were conceived in the military. In the army, line refers to the generals down through the officer ranks, to non-commissioned grades of sergeant and corporal, to the privates in the infantry, all of whom are directly involved in military engagement. Staff officers, on the other hand, are technical and planning support experts who advise senior line officers, but who do not engage in direct military activities themselves.

Line employees in organisations are all those either directly engaged in the core work of the business, or in the organisational chain of command, directing and supervising the work of those directly doing the core work of the business. On this basis, line employees include the chief executive right down to the most junior operative or sales person.

Staff employees, on the other hand, are those employees supporting, advising and administering the work of the line employees, e.g. internal auditors, public relations advisors, human resources specialists, and so on (Fayol 1949).

As long as a firm remains small and relatively simple, managers can exercise effective control in the organisation, based solely on line relationships. However, as an organisation grows, it is likely to need some specialist support, e.g. an accountant, human resources specialist or public relations advisor. These staff support activities, while important, are not part of the firm's core competency business activities such as engineering, manufacturing or sales. Staff departments only propose, recommend, advise or assist other departments in their work. They generally lack the power and authority to insist that their advice be adhered to. Staff employees generally operate through 'expert' power, which refers to the ability of a staff specialist to influence and persuade based on their expert knowledge and skill in a particular field. A staff advisor may also be able to use 'legitimate' power, where specific powers may be delegated to them, e.g. where a safety officer is delegated the power to shut down an unsafe machine.

Mintzberg (1979) distinguished five basic parts of organisational structure: *strategic apex* (senior executive management), *middle line* (e.g. operations middle management), *operating core* (e.g. operations personnel), *technostructure* (e.g technical expertise) and *support staff* (e.g. finance). In Mintzberg's framework, the collection of the strategic apex together with the middle line and the operating core can be collectively described as the line organisation, which we discussed earlier. His category of support staff is clearly staff personnel, also as discussed above, who provide expert advisory and administrative support. The final group Mintzberg introduces is the technostructure. This is an important group, who provide the engineering and technical expertise to the firm. The group may include research and development engineers and chemists, software development personnel, and other engineering and technical personnel.

Today, there is a clearly observable trend towards integrating some of the staff roles (e.g. corporate marketing) into the business unit activity; out-sourcing other staff roles (e.g. IT support); and dismantling others altogether (e.g. corporate strategic planning). Galbraith and Lawler warn that 'the reality is that most organisations cannot afford large, centralised staff groups. They particularly cannot afford them if the staff groups become insulated from the business, fail to look critically at the value they add to the business, and are not responsive to business needs' (1993: 82).

Centralisation and Decentralisation

Centralisation and decentralisation should be seen as polarities on a continuum of the level of authority delegated down through the organisation. This concept is not about geographic dispersion of business units; rather, centralisation and decentralisation is about who gets to make certain decisions and controls certain resources. Centralisation refers to the concentration of authority and responsibility for decision making in the hands of only the most senior executives at the top of an organisation's hierarchy. It then follows that decentralisation refers to authority and responsibility for decision making being dispersed downwards to operating unit managers and below.

Most organisational experts recommend that decisions should be made:

- as far down the organisation as people are capable of making such a decision;
- by those who have the correct information upon which to make decisions; and
- as close to the customer as possible, for maximum responsiveness to their needs.

Theory & Practice

The mail-order company, LL Bean, delegates substantial authority to their customer service representatives in order to allow them to quickly respond to and satisfactorily address customer complaints, without having to refer proposed solutions upwards for approval, which delays the resolution of the complaint. This approach has resulted in LL Bean being recognised globally not only for their high quality products but also for their highly responsive customer service.

Davis and Weckler noted that Hewlett Packard in the 1980s had thirty-eight central committees that supervised most major aspects of the company: 'This structure slowed down the company's ability to react to changes in their competitive environment. Recognising this, in 1990 the company dissolved these committees and decentralised most of the authority to the divisions' (1996: 72). Delegating responsibility to the individual business units allowed those businesses to respond much more quickly and effectively to opportunities and challenges in their respective business environments.

Naturally, there are advantages to both centralisation and decentralisation. Advantages of centralisation include:

- A greater uniformity of policies, procedures and decision making, providing greater consistency in decision making.
- Critical scarce resources (e.g. funding, management talent, and so on) can be applied to the place of greatest need in the organisation.
- Knowledge and innovation are more likely to be shared within and across the organisation.
- Middle level managers do not have to be as skilled (or therefore as well-paid) as all important decisions are referred upwards.

- Independence at the unit level is avoided as is excessive inter-unit rivalry and competition, because top-level management make all the decisions and do not allow excessive rivalry between the business units.

The advantages of decentralisation include:

- Local decision making avoids clogging senior management with continuous, relatively minor decision making, freeing them for more important, longer-term strategic focus and planning.
- Decisions are made at a level where most information is available on the issue.
- The organisation can respond more quickly to local customers and conditions (this is further developed in discussions on geographic structures in Chapter 3).
- There is the potential to stimulate greater independence and creativity at the local level.
- Local managers have a higher level of motivation and ownership of responsibility when they are entrusted to make decisions.

Obviously, the advantages of centralisation represent the disadvantages of decentralisation and vice versa.

Huczynski and Buchanan (2001) point out that organisations regularly swing from decentralisation to centralisation and back again. They explain that these swings are in response to changes in company size and developing market opportunities. They further suggest that a swing towards centralisation may occur for no other reason than an incoming new chief executive wishing to make a highly visible impact on the managers, employees, shareholders and financial analysts.

Theory & Practice

Black & Decker had twenty-five manufacturing plants in thirteen countries, selling into fifty countries. Each business division operated quite independently. The Italian division made power tools for the Italian market; the British division made power tools for the British market, and so on. As a result, successful

> *products in one country took years to be introduced in others. At one point, eight different design centres were producing 260 different motors. A worldwide recession and earnings slippage in the 1980s forced the company to fundamentally change its decentralisation policy. After that, motors were standardised. Local operations could change some features for local market tastes but retained the product's fundamental (and standardised) design (Hellreigel et al. 1998:1).*

Today, levels of centralisation and decentralisation in international companies are varied and dynamic. Some organisations are decentralising; others are centralising. Some organisations are decentralising but are providing some minimum guiding principles on such issues as business ethics, financial requirements and human resources practices. Some organisations have coined the expression 'glocal', which suggests that they operate a hybrid whereby they have important global policies but also accept the need to amend some of these to take account of local legislation, custom and practice. BP operates a business model of 'centralised direction and decentralised implementation'. Their strategic objectives and values are shared throughout the group but implementation is through empowerment at the operational unit level. The company operates based on a set of clearly established principles, sharing of best practice and extensive communication.

Another hybrid of the centralisation/decentralisation continuum is one whereby an organisation decentralises their businesses by product groupings or divisions, but centralises their manufacturing operations in order to achieve enhanced production economies of scale and provide a superior supply chain. These hybrids are discussed and explored in Chapter 6.

Conclusion

In this chapter we have discussed many of the fundamentals of organisation design: bureaucracy and Taylorism; chain of command; layers of hierarchy; spans of control; line and staff relationships and the centralisation/decentralisation continuum. Many of these tend to be interrelated: narrow spans tend to create tall structures and centralised decision making; broad spans, on the other hand, go with flatter hierarchy and more decentralised decision making. It is important to understand and appreciate these fundamentals of structure before beginning to discuss and explore some of the newer and ever-evolving models and hybrids in the following chapters.

In concluding this chapter, the reader might consider completing an analysis of the layers and spans of control in their own organisation and, if possible, benchmarking their organisation against one or more relevant organisations.

Case Based on Chapter 2

Eastern Technologies, based in Nashua, New Hampshire, USA, designs, markets and manufactures speciality HiFi audio speakers including a new range of speakers for Apple iPods and other MP3 personal audio equipment. These speakers allow iPods and similar products to be 'docked' and then reproduce high-fidelity audio. Eastern's sales have soared in recent years, having 'piggy-backed' on the extraordinary success of personal music systems. Competitors include Apple, Bose, B&O and Logitech.

In order to cater for their growth, Eastern established an off-shore manufacturing facility in Taiwan in 2003. The Taiwanese operation now employs 300 employees, 20 miles south of Taipei. The operation is managed by a US expatriate, Mike Chen, but all other employees are locals. Up until now, the Taiwan plant had an organisational structure of just four layers: general manager, department managers, production and test supervisors, and assembly and test operatives. Spans of control are an average of 1:30. The operation runs a single-day shift, Monday to Friday.

The Situation

Last week, Doug Jablonski, vice president of manufacturing in New Hampshire, received a personnel requisition from the Taiwanese General Manager Mike Chen to hire two new production supervisors. The reason for these new personnel requisitions is that Taiwan management plan to promote two existing supervisors to a new grade of assistant production manager positions. These new positions would report to the production manager and each would have four production supervisors reporting to them.

In the documentation supporting this requisition, Chen explains that the reasons for the proposed promotions and consequent replacements are:

- production levels are at an all-time high and the production manager badly needs additional resources to cope with demand;
- the proposed appointees to the new positions are excellent in their current roles and this would be a very positive message not only to them but to the rest of the plant;
- these new positions would provide good 'back-up' as production managers 'in training'.

During a subsequent conference call to discuss this request and other manufacturing issues, General Manager Chen also explained that these two supervisors had offers of similar positions from another technology assembly plant down the street.

This proposal presents Jablonski with something of a dilemma. His Taiwan general manager has generally delivered on all his production goals and, despite significant growth, manages a relatively trouble-free operation in a different time zone, on the other side of the world. On the other hand, Jablonski is uncomfortable with the idea of adding an extra layer into what should be a relatively straightforward and flat structure. He is less concerned about cost, given local labour costs, and more concerned about the possible implications of a taller structure on local communication, role clarity and decision making.

Given the strong performance of the Taiwan operation up to now, Jablonski has not turned down many of Chen's requests and is uncertain about how best to reply to this request.

Questions

1. What is your analysis of the situation? What are the options open to Jablonski?
2. Which option would you select and why?

CHAPTER 3

FUNCTIONAL, GEOGRAPHIC AND DIVISIONAL STRUCTURES

Introduction

Traditionally, most commercial firms have been organised by functional speciality, geographic national boundaries or divisional product lines. Chapter 3 examines each of these structures and considers the advantages and disadvantages of each.

It is important to note, however, that these structural choices are not mutually exclusive, and evolving organisation designs are likely to have some elements of all three. Such hybrid structures are explored in detail in Chapter 6.

1. Functional Structures

A functional organisational structure is organised on the basis of specialised functions or departments – such as marketing, sales, production, finance, engineering, and so on (see Figure 3.1 for an

Figure 3.1: Example of a Functional Organisation

CEO				
VP Sales & Marketing	VP R&D	VP Manufacturing	VP Finance	VP Human Resources
All Sales and Marketing Personnel and Activities	All R&D Personnel and Activities	All Manufacturing Personnel and Activities	All Financial Personnel and Activities	All HR Personnel and Activities

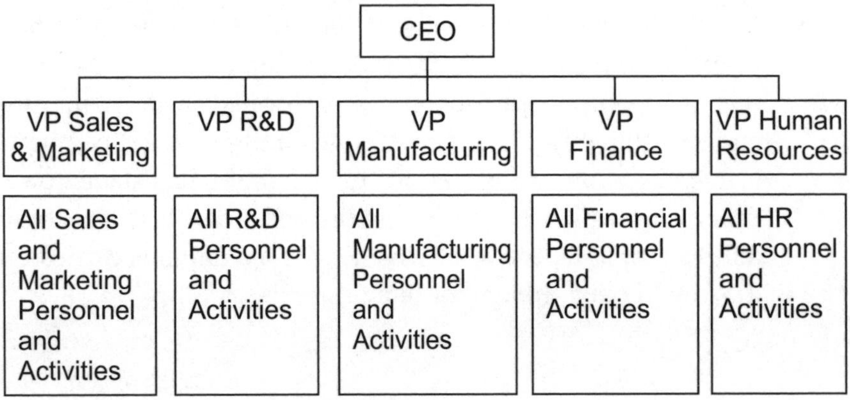

example of a simple functional structure). Functions, in turn, can be further subdivided into sub-functions or processes. Finance, for example, can be subdivided into financial accounting, taxation, accounts payable and payroll. Typically, firms start out as functional structures. It is the most basic form of organisation design, and is often a starting point from which other forms of structure evolve.

A functional structure typically provides advantages of clarity, scale and opportunities for specialisation:

- There is clarity in the assignment of responsibilities both inside and outside of the organisation. People tend to understand each other's roles and responsibilities.
- The functional expertise is pooled in one department. The scale of the pooled resources presents an opportunity to build a deeper functional knowledge and specialisation and, potentially, a core competency.
- The clustering of the same functional experts together and typically co-locating them in one area or department greatly facilitates the transfer of knowledge and ideas among and between the members.
- A functional structure allows the presentation of a single face to the external world: the marketing manager presents a single face to the customer, the purchasing manager to the supplier, and so on.
- The pooled resources of a functional department are more likely to be able to finance a specialist individual such as a specialist technologist or advisor.
- Galbraith notes that a functional organisational structure both promotes standardisation and reduces duplication: 'An activity that is organised functionally is performed in the same way and (presumably) in the best way throughout the company' (2002: 24). Intel Corporation, for example, has standardised processes, which have been optimised and must be strictly adhered to, irrespective of whether the operation is carried out in New Mexico, Ireland or Israel.

A functional structure is more likely to be effective where there is little or no complexity, e.g. where it has a single or few product offerings for a few customers, and where the environment is relatively stable.

Increasingly, organisations are finding distinct disadvantages when they are structured in functional silos. (Functional structures are sometimes referred to as silo organisations because they can sometimes look like sets of stacks or stovepipes on a hierarchical organisational chart. The term silo is also used to depict a store of similar functional capabilities, stored in one area.) The disadvantages of functional silos include:

- Potential for a slow response, where there is need for coordination and collaboration across departments. Issues are referred upwards for resolution, overloading more senior managers. Decisions pile up and top managers do not respond quickly enough (Daft 2001).
- New product introductions and innovation generally are slower because of poor coordination and information sharing across functional silos. There are often barriers between different departments, inhibiting collaboration and teamwork. The sporting analogy of a relay race has been used to depict the slower stage-by-stage process, where each department completes its work before it is handed over to the next phase of development.
- Under such a structure, for example, a micro-chip designer would complete all the necessary circuit design before handing it over to the software development engineers to write the code to test the part in production. Only then would it be handed over to production to figure out the solid state physics of how to make it!
- Referred to as concurrent engineering, new product development teams include circuit designers, test systems development engineers and manufacturing personnel, who collectively manage the entire new product introduction process from beginning to end, their individual competencies and responsibilities blurring as they work on the entire process

together. BMW now physically co-locate its design engineers and manufacturing engineers together around developing prototypes. Such essential collaboration is unlikely in a traditional functional structure.

- Managers and employees often lack a clear understanding of how their work contributes to the performance of the organisation as a whole. They can easily have a restricted view of strategic goals. In functional structures, the focus of goal setting tends to be departmental in nature and is often not well integrated at the top of the organisation. In addition, departments will compete and fight with each other for their share of scarce budgetary resources.

In general, functional structures are declining in popularity because of the disadvantages outlined above. In many industries, speed and agility are more important than scale and responsiveness as a condition for survival (Galbraith 2002).

2. Geographic Structures

Country or regional structures are used by some global organisations as their primary business units to manage and coordinate their businesses around the world. As organisational structure choices are not mutually exclusive, it is possible to have a functional structure within a geographic region.

A geographic structure, as its name suggests, is the combination of activities required to serve a substantial regional market and be managed from that region or country. This structure can be applied as easily to a country's regions, e.g. (US) East Coast, Mid-West and West Coast, as to continental regions such as Asia/Pacific (APAC), Europe/Middle East/Africa (EMEA) and the Americas (see Figure 3.2).

Theory & Practice

Many international firms use geographic structures to address regional and cultural differences and exploit unique market opportunities in those regions. For example, Kendall Healthcare Products established a German subsidiary to manufacture locally in Germany and market a broad line

---

of products developed in the United States for German consumption. In this case, localised manufacturing made sense because healthcare product standards and regulatory requirements vary considerably from country to country (Morrison et al. 1991).

Figure 3.2: Example of a Geographical Organisational Structure

CEO		
Americas	**EMEA**	**APAC**
USA	UK	Japan
Canada	France	Philippines
South America	Germany	Australia
Mexico & Caribbean	Turkey	New Zealand
	Nigeria	South Korea

Industries such as coal and highway construction need to be near sources of supply such as mines and quarries. Equally, industries that have high product transportation costs should be close to their marketplace.

The advantages and opportunities of a geographic structure include the following:

- The ability to exploit unique market opportunities because of cultural or regulatory requirements (see Kendall Healthcare above).
- Senior management operates closer to markets and customers, and in the same time zone. The structure decentralises decision making, at least to some extent.
- Sales people are nearer to their customers and can spend more time selling and less time traveling.

- Transportation cost savings where the cost of raw material or finished product transportation is a significant proportion of total costs.
- The ability to adapt to regional differences in both products and services.
- Customer service: there is a local 'face' for customers.

The disadvantages of a geographic structure include:

- The economies of scale enjoyed by the functional structure (discussed above) are likely to be diminished.
- The disadvantages of a decentralised structure also apply, including less corporate control and coordination. It is very difficult if not impossible for service providers (such as accountancy firms), who are geographically structured under country managers with local profit centres, to provide global clients with a timely and consistent service across all the countries in which the client operates.
- Local management may emphasise and overly focus on their own geographically based needs and goals at the expense of the greater good of the corporation.
- It is at least possible that some regional managers come to see their geographic area as their personal fiefdoms and have been known to want to expand their political domain. For example, a country manager with only a local sales activity tries to persuade the corporation of the need to have local manufacturing for no other reason but to expand his or her local operation. A similar example is where a corporation decides to set up a local manufacturing activity and the existing country sales manager sets claim to the new facility on the basis that he or she is the so-called country manager, despite the fact that they have little if any experience and competence in managing a manufacturing facility. Some regional managers see their employee talent pool as theirs; chattels never to be offered up for the greater corporate good. With talent locked up in country or regional silos, corporations find it difficult to identify and relocate talent to where it is most urgently needed (Collings *et al.* 2008).

It is fair to say that some of the disadvantages outlined above are more to do with decentralisation than geographic structures per se. Organisations such as GE, Procter & Gamble and Unilever operate regional structures but with a high level of centralised policies and procedures around talent management. In Unilever, all managers worldwide are considered a corporate resource and are managed and developed accordingly (Boxhall and Purcell 2003).

Today, information technology is making location less important (Friedman 2005). Companies such as Dell sell over the Internet to customers. A customer service call to many European suppliers today is as likely to be routed through to a customer service desk in Bangalore or Islamabad. As IT makes our world a smaller place, it seems that more and more corporations are moving away from pure geographic structures to more hybrid arrangements. This does not mean that corporations will not expand into emerging geographic sectors (e.g. Beijing); but the focus will be on market development and/or a low cost manufacturing opportunity. How they structure the business opportunity is more likely to be embedded in a business unit or a hybrid 'front-back' structure, which is discussed later.

3. Divisional Product Line or Strategic Business Unit (SBU) Structure

When a company with a functional structure begins to expand its product lines in any significant way, the resulting increased organisational complexity severely tests the old functional structure. A response to this increased complexity for many companies is to reorganise and restructure by product family or market. Typically, when Hewlett Packard or 3M introduce a new product and that product or product family reaches an efficient scale of manufacturing, they spawn a new business unit or division to develop that product with its own management, product development, marketing, and manufacturing or service provision. Hewlett Packard, GE, 3M and PepsiCo all organise their corporation primarily along business unit or market structures. For example, Procter & Gamble, the $56 billion consumer products corporation, is organised under detergents, paper products, personal care, and so on.

An example of a divisional product line or strategic business unit is shown in Figure 3.3.

Figure 3.3: Example of a Strategic Business Unit (SBU)

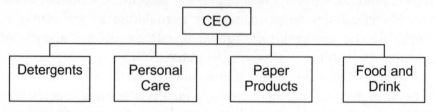

The advantages of a strategic business unit organisational structure include:

- It reduces the organisational complexity facing an organisation. In effect, this structure creates a collection of smaller organisations, dedicated to particular businesses.
- Most importantly, the unique needs of each market and the customers in that marketplace are better understood and served.
- Unprofitable product lines are easier to identify.
- Product structures facilitate strategies of product diversification and new product development. To create a new product, management creates a new division (Galbraith 2002).
- If an organisation decides to sell a business, the product structure more easily facilitates the spinning off of that business.
- This structure can also more easily facilitate the acquisition of another business.

Disadvantages of the business unit or market structure include:

- There is very real potential to create individual business silos that actively compete with each other rather than with external competition. In 2005, Howard Stringer, CEO of Sony, launched his 'Sony United' initiative to try to break down the silo walls between the group's notoriously independent divisions. Philips was another example of a large organisation operating as a set of quite disparate companies acting independently of each other. Previously, as long as divisions achieved their 'bottom line', no one cared about collaboration or group-level profitability. In 2001, Chief Executive Kleisterlee initiated their 'Towards One Philips' (TOP) programme to unify the organisation and promote greater cooperation and support. This programme yielded significant success as exemplified by the introduction of new healthcare equipment, which was the outcome of collaboration between their medical, lighting and consumer electronics divisions.

- Another significant difficulty is how best to manage customers who buy products from more than one division. Companies like Hewlett Packard typically do not want to purchase from several different divisional suppliers from around the world. Not unreasonably, they want to have a single point of contact with their supplier. Some organisations have responded to this situation by appointing 'lead divisions' that might 'purchase' supplies from other divisions on an inter-company basis and then be able to provide that single source of supply to the customer.

- There is a very real danger that splitting up an R&D or engineering team and spreading them across the various divisions will create a serious fragmentation of a critical core competency. Where such key resources are spread across divisions, it is essential that there are effective lateral integrating mechanisms to share knowledge and foster innovation.

- Similar to the geographic structure, there is the danger that, unless explicitly managed, division managers see their personnel resources as just that – theirs! GE, Unilever and Procter & Gamble go to great lengths to manage up-and-coming management talent as a collective global corporate resource.

- There is a danger that economies of scale will diminish. This can happen where each division owns its own manufacturing and/or where each division negotiates its own contract for critical supplies.

- There is a great temptation on the part of divisional general managers to have direct control over all their resources. Replicating such resources in each division creates significant duplication of resources and missed opportunities to share scarce resources.

The last two disadvantages can be overcome by using some form of hybrid structure, e.g. centralising manufacturing and making it a centralised service provider to the product lines. Other services can also be centralised for economies of scale and avoidance of duplication, including IT, finance, purchasing, human resources, and so on.

Mintzberg (1979) raises some interesting questions about whether or not certain contingencies influence structure design. His hypothesis includes: older organisations have more formalised structures and behaviours; the structure reflects the age of foundation of the industry; the larger the organisation, the more elaborate its structure and specialised its tasks; the larger the organisation, the larger the size of its average unit; the larger the unit, the more formal its behaviour. He concludes on the contingency factors of age:

> Structures do not seem to change continuously or in linear patterns; it seems more accurate to describe them as passing through distinct transitions, fundamental changes in the way their work is divided and coordinated (248).

Mintzberg's view that the age of the organisation is likely to have an influence on organisational structure is well borne out in the contrast between Ryanair's structure and the traditional airline flag carriers of Europe, e.g. Alitalia, Air France and Aer Lingus. In an interview with the *Wall Street Journal,* Ryanair's Chief Executive Michael O'Leary stated:

> We keep the management structure extremely flat. As we grow, we're only adding aircraft, pilots, inflight people and engineers. We don't need these layers of bureaucracy or layers of management.... So, hopefully, we'll avoid the bull by keeping our feet on the ground and not losing the run of ourselves. The downside of success that we really worry about is the danger that the more successful you are, the more likely you are to lose sight of the things that made you successful. (Ruddock 2007: 267)

Professional services companies including accounting firms and actuarial consultancies acquire suitable local firms in new geographies to expand their service geographic reach. Some of these acquisitions were structured initially as country entities, with local managers. Increasingly, however, such firms are restructured by global product lines in order to provide seamless services to multinational clients across country boundaries. Some accounting firms operate a hybrid structure where the organisation is really an international coordinating entity for its autonomous country member firms with a common brand, philosophy, technologies and practice methods. Under this arrangement, member firms maintain a strong country focus and structure and support multinational clients through service level agreements.

Conclusion

This chapter considered functional, geographic and product line business unit structures and their respective advantages and disadvantages. Some of the disadvantages can be addressed by hybrid structures and by linking or reinforcing mechanisms. What is clear is that whatever structure is selected should be regularly examined for continuing relevance to the strategy.

At this point, the reader might consider completing an analysis of their organisation or an organisation that they know well. Is the organisation structured by function, geography or product line? In the analysis, identify the structural advantages and disadvantages of this particular organisation design.

Case Based on Chapter 3

Michael Ryan realised that he was going to have to face up to changing the way he managed his business, Liffey Vale Food Products plc. Michael was promoted to the position of managing director of Liffey Vale a couple of years ago. Despite his best efforts over the past two years, the business has remained sluggish, and he has come to the conclusion that 'more of the same' isn't going to fundamentally change the company's fortunes in the years ahead.

Company Background

Liffey Vale Food Products plc is a public limited company, listed on the Dublin stock exchange. Headquarters are based in Kildare town in the heartland of Ireland. The company has three milk processing manufacturing plants within a sixty mile radius of Kildare. It also has a poultry meat processing plant 100 miles south of Kildare. In 2006, Liffey Vale had an annual dairy foods turnover of almost €500 million in commodity cheese, butter and powder ingredients (whey and caseins). Turnover in poultry products was €80 million for the same period.

While the dairy business is generally profitable, the poultry business has been running at a loss for the past three years. Ryan believes that 'the poultry business is borderline breakeven at best; and it would require significant investment to achieve even that position.'

The dairy operation sells all its butter and packaged cheddar cheese under the retailers' brand to a number of UK and Irish supermarket chains. It sells bulk cheese to its UK subsidiary; and whey and casein powders to Irish and UK nutritional products and baby food manufacturers. The balance of its butter and cheese production is bought by the Irish Dairy Board, which is an Irish government-sponsored national cooperative that markets Irish dairy products under the Irish Dairy Board brand internationally.

Liffey Vale has a highly successful UK-based operation in Kent, which blends and packages speciality cheeses as primary ingredients for pizza manufacturers and hamburger chains. The UK division has rapidly expanded its sales operation into Germany, the Netherlands, Spain and Portugal. The UK operation uses commodity cheese produced in the Irish facilities but also sources cheese locally in the UK if the price is more attractive. In 2003, the company bought a dairy foods business in Wisconsin, USA. The intent behind this acquisition was to try and mirror the UK business model and its achievements. While it is still a little early to judge, the US division hasn't yet excited its new owners. However, Ryan and his executive board are convinced that this acquisition and business model will pay good dividends into the future. The company also has two promising joint ventures: one in Argentina and one in South Africa.

The company has had a functional organisational structure since its inception as a farmer's cooperative over seventy years ago. The top management team includes the managing director, financial controller, three dairy plant general managers and the poultry plant manager, head of the UK/Europe operations, and head of the US operations, together with the heads of sales (retail and Irish Dairy Board), R&D, quality and HR.

Michael Ryan's Concerns and Considerations

Ryan believes that there is a strong and historical bias towards manufacturing and dairy science excellence throughout most of the company. After all, the company was originally set up as a farmers' cooperative to process their milk and 'find a home' for the produce. Ryan is concerned that there is insufficient marketing and customer focus in their individual thinking and in their collective discussions at meetings. He is also concerned that as they move further into product niches, they do not have the necessary market and product expertise in each of these very different markets. He is also pessimistic about the future of the poultry business as it has very limited scale. He wonders if he should sell that business and knows there are a couple of interested would-be purchasers out there. Personally, he is also finding it increasingly difficult to carve out time for important strategy development as it seems he is drawn into so many operational issues and too often has to play 'referee' between manufacturing and sales.

Over many conversations with his HR manager, Helen Murphy, and from observing some of his bigger dairy products competitors, Kerry Group, Dairygold, Dairy Crest and Glanbia, Ryan now believes that he needs to reorganise the company in such a way as to give substantial focus to his markets and customers. Recently he held an executive off-site meeting where he presented his concerns and sought reaction and suggestions from the group. After some robust exchanges of views, a consensus emerged that some reorganisation might be warranted around markets, products and services. The executive group agreed to work together as a team over the following six months to design, develop and plan the implementation of a new organisational structure. Ryan stressed that the success of this major organisational change was less about the quest to find the perfect structure and much more to do with getting a much closer and sharper focus on markets, and industrial and end customers.

Annual Revenues:
2004 – €556 million
2005 – €568 million
2006 – €580 million

2006 Sales by Market

Retailer branded butter and cheese, UK and Ireland:	€225 million
UK/Europe cheese supplies to manufacturers:	€175 million
US cheese supplies to manufacturers:	€50 million
Whey and casein powders to manufacturers:	€25 million
Joint ventures:	€10 million
Irish Dairy Board:	€15 million
Poultry:	€80 million
Total:	€580 million

Questions

1. From an organisation design perspective, describe the key organisational issues that need to be addressed.
2. Would you restructure Liffey Vale? If yes, how would you restructure the company? Are there risks that need to be addressed?

CHAPTER 4

MATRIX STRUCTURES

Introduction

Given the ever-increasing complexity in organisations, it is hardly surprising that there are conflicting objectives and priorities. In addition, organisations, no matter how well-designed vertically, have critical lateral interdependencies across major departments which need to be managed efficiently. In order to balance conflicting objectives and these lateral interdependencies, many organisations have introduced matrix or dual reporting structures. The unique characteristics of a matrix structure are that *two* structures (functional, product business unit or geography) are superimposed and integrated on two axes. Under this structure, a geography leader and a functional leader have equal authority and employees in that geography and function report simultaneously on both axes (see Figure 4.1).

Figure 4.1: A Sample Matrix Organisational Structure

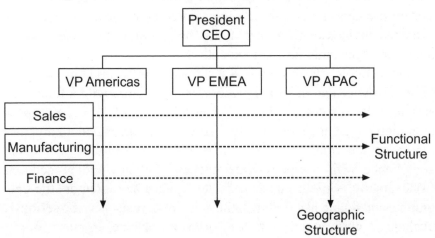

This chapter discusses the concept of matrix management; analyses its strengths and weaknesses; suggests that the essence of matrix is not structure but a 'frame of mind'; and presents concepts of primary and secondary reporting relationships.

Matrix Management

An example of a matrix of responsibilities between a product division leader and a geography leader would be:

Product leader – develops and delivers the global strategy for that product line; ensures the global delivery of products and services; achieves sales targets and budgets; generates new products for global markets; decides whether to enter or exit markets; actively cooperates with geography in attracting, developing and retaining personnel talent.
Geography leader – develops and delivers a geographic strategy that integrates product offerings from product divisions for own geographical area (presents one face to the customer); achieves sales targets and budgets; fosters and grows customer relationships; ensures compliance with local laws and customs; cooperates with product divisions in attracting, developing and retaining personnel talent.

Huczynski and Buchanan (2001) credit TRW with introducing the first matrix structure in 1957. TRW found that traditional functional or product groupings were ineffective in managing the technological and manufacturing complexity in their joint military-industrial missile system projects. These projects were so complex, and ran over such extended periods of time that it was not possible to make a single manager responsible for their execution.

In its simplest form, Figure 4.2 shows a matrix structure designed to both balance and integrate a geographic structure with a functional structure. In this case, a financial controller reports to the European operation's vice president on regional financial management and also reports to the chief financial officer of the company to ensure full compliance with company-wide financial policies and procedures. Conceptually, while it makes sense to balance and integrate the geographic and financial structures, the concept of matrix can be seriously challenged when goals conflict or priorities change. In our example, imagine that the financial controller is responsible for the introduction of a new payroll system locally, while at the same time is a member of a corporate team involved in the introduction of an enterprise-wide management information system (e.g. SAP). What happens to the local payroll initiative when the priority rating of the corporate-wide system becomes very urgent and requires additional resources? How does the local operations vice president react, when his controller advises that he has to delay the introduction of the payroll system locally in order to support the enterprise-wide system? How can these competing priorities be reconciled? How does the local controller keep both of his or her bosses satisfied? In another example, corporate HR may want the divisional HR manager to toe the corporate line, but the same HR manager may be under pressure from the division vice president to focus on his/her particular needs and priorities (see Figure 4.2).

**Figure 4.2: A Matrix Organisational Structure
Balancing Geographic and Functional (Finance) Structures**

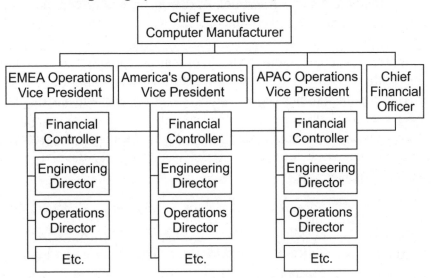

Strengths and Weaknesses of Matrix Management

Strengths include:

• The matrix dual-authority structure helps and facilitates communication and coordination across key constituencies, e.g. product divisions, geographies, functions, and so on.

- Scarce resources (e.g. technical talent) can be shared across a number of product divisions as projects come and go.
- It is suited to complex decision making in dynamically changing situations.

The weaknesses and difficulties of a matrix structure include:

- Without excellent communication between the dual senior managers, employees will find goal setting and priorities confusing and frustrating, potentially leading to excessive stress and diminished work quality.
- It can be cumbersome, time-consuming and costly, and involve planning, communication meetings, and conflict resolution in goal-setting and priorities.
- Matrix structure has the potential to get out of hand, where employees end up not just with two but with multiple reporting relationships, each additional relationship adding exponentially to complexity and confusion.

There is no doubt about the need for matrix type structures in many organisations to provide greater integration and to support important cross-departmental interdependencies. However, for matrix structures to be successful there needs to be a very high level of collaborative behaviour, processes to support the matrix, and senior managers who have the necessary interpersonal skills and actively develop those skills and behaviours:

	Sensible	Culture of	Systems	Leaders with
Effective =	Matrix $\times$	Collaborative $\times$	to Support $\times$	Skills and
Matrix	Structure	Behaviour	The Matrix	Inclination
	Design			

In establishing matrix organisations, companies usually achieve the first element of the design, namely the structure design. However, too many companies fail to put the other elements in place: development of a collaborative culture; processes to support the matrix; and effective leadership behaviours. The results of that failure can be political gamesmanship, confusing priorities and stress at both organisational and individual levels. This is reflected in Hellriegel *et al.* (1998), who warn that clarity of reporting direction is at the core of the chain of command and suggest that no subordinate should receive orders from more than one supervisor. These authors indicate that, without unity of command, instructions will be both cloudy and confusing. Mintzberg (1979) cautions that matrix structures sacrifice the principles of unity of command. He suggests that dispensing with the principle of unity of command creates relationships that require highly developed inter-personal skills and considerable tolerance for ambiguity; and such an environment is no place for those seeking total clarity, stability and a stress-free environment. When a matrixed employee's managers do not agree on goal priorities or have different value systems, the employee often does not know how to behave and ends up caught in the middle. The decision regarding whom to pay attention to is usually made on political grounds rather than in the best interests of the organisation (Ackoff 1994).

'Matrix is not Structure'

In their highly influential article, Bartlett and Ghoshal (1990) suggest that the obvious solution to strategies that require multiple, simultaneous management capabilities is the matrix structure. They propose that the matrix parallel reporting relationships acknowledges the diverse, often conflicting needs of functional, product and geographic management groups, and provides a formal mechanism to reconcile conflicting issues and needs. However, the authors apply a useful medical metaphor to warn of the dangers of defining the organisation in purely structural terms:

> The term formal structure describes only the organisation's basic anatomy. Companies must also concern themselves with organisational physiology – the systems and relationships that allow the lifeblood of information to flow through the organisation. They also need to develop a healthy organisation psychology – the shared norms, values and beliefs that shape the way individual managers think and act. (3)

The authors warn that when some companies announce their formal structures, they hope that the very announcement will force changes in interpersonal relationships and decision-making processes, which in turn will reshape the individual attitudes and actions of managers. For those wishful companies, nothing could be further from reality. The authors stress the need to develop that organisational psychology of collaboration and support and wisely suggest that 'matrix is not structure but a frame of mind.'

Mindful of that organisational psychology, behaviours that support a matrix include:

- jointly developing and committing to shared goals;
- leading the organisation by influence rather than authority;
- explicitly clarifying roles, goals and priorities;
- sharing in decisions about the performance and promotions of jointly matrixed managers;
- dealing early and effectively with priority conflicts that will undoubtedly arise in the course of the review period.

On the other hand, behaviours that damage a matrix structure include:

- a matrix manager focusing selfishly on his/her own goals at the expense of the other matrix manager, and communicating little with the other manager;
- setting goals and priorities for matrixed employees who report to them, without reference to other managers to whom the employees also report;
- completing performance or promotion decisions for employees, without reference to other managers to whom the employees also report.

Theory & Practice
Matrix management is very clever in theory but very difficult in practice. To illustrate the difficulty of matrix structures being cumbersome and time-consuming, Ashkenas and his colleagues (2002) cited Digital Equipment Corporation (DEC), which

was one of the best known examples of a matrix organisation throughout the 1980s. Digital's matrix called for high levels of involvement and engagement in decision making across the company. Every decision required a committee and intense consultation back and forth between product groups, functions and geographies. Outsiders were often left with the curiosity that everyone seemed to be involved yet no one appeared to be accountable. The difficulty arose across the company where people expected to be consulted on everything, which allowed individuals and functions to stonewall, making agreement on major programmes and strategic directions very difficult. As a result of continuous consultation and endless debate, Digital was unable to move fast enough to keep up with its industry. In 1998, Compaq purchased DEC, and the latter essentially went out of business.

A consultative, matrixed structure offers clear advantages in organisational coordination. However, it is essential that it is supported by processes that reconcile priorities, differences of opinion and conflicts quickly and effectively.

Primary and Secondary Reporting Relationships in Matrix Structures

It is a common practice in some matrixed organisations today to identify one or another axis of the matrix as the primary reporting relationship. This primary reporting relationship is typically represented on an organisational chart as a solid line and the secondary relationship is represented as a broken or dotted line. In many organisations, the line of business will have the primary relationship, with the function having the secondary or 'dotted-line' relationship. In the example in Figure 4.3, the European financial controller has a primary reporting relationship with the European operation's vice president and has a secondary reporting relationship with the chief financial officer (CFO). In this scenario, the European controller reports on a primary basis to the regional business executive for all operational matters and reports on a secondary basis to the CFO for group financial policies and procedures.

There are also organisations that have key functions such as finance and human resources reporting on a primary (straight line) basis to the head of the function and on a secondary (dotted line) basis to the head of the business or region. This is often done for corporate control and, in some instances, for shared services opportunities. Whether reporting relationships have equal weighting or have solid and dotted line arrangements, the same advantages and reservations of matrix management apply.

**Figure 4.3: Matrix Structure
[Showing Primary (Solid Line) and Secondary (Dotted Line)]**

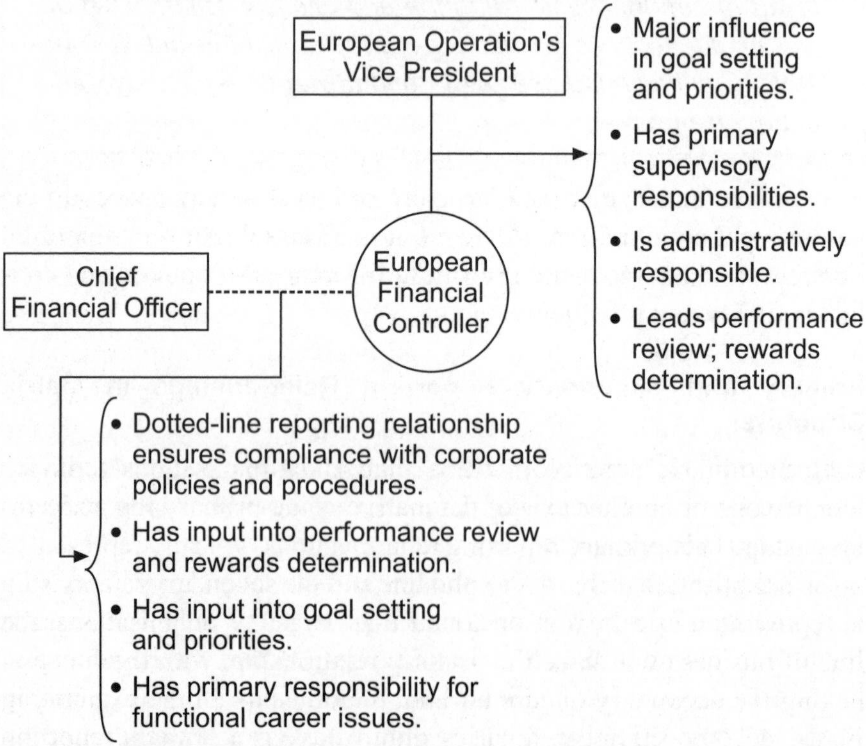

European Operation's Vice President

- Major influence in goal setting and priorities.
- Has primary supervisory responsibilities.
- Is administratively responsible.
- Leads performance review; rewards determination.

Chief Financial Officer

European Financial Controller

- Dotted-line reporting relationship ensures compliance with corporate policies and procedures.
- Has input into performance review and rewards determination.
- Has input into goal setting and priorities.
- Has primary responsibility for functional career issues.

Conclusion

In conclusion, Bartlett and Ghoshal's observations seem appropriate:

The in-built conflict in a matrix structure pulls managers in several directions at once. Developing a matrix of flexible perspectives and relationships within each manager's mind, however, achieves an entirely different result. It lets individuals make the judgements and negotiate the trade-offs that drive the organisation towards a shared strategic objective. (1990:8)

Matrix is not really about structure, it is indeed about a frame of mind, and the real challenge is to achieve that frame of mind among and between all the key players. A matrix structure certainly has the potential to facilitate coordination and support interdependencies across the different constituencies, but it needs critically important elements including a culture of collaborative teamwork, processes to reconcile priority conflicts quickly, and visible and supportive leadership.

Case Based on Chapter 4

Charles Ingham was delighted. He had just finished a call from Rich Hardy in Atlanta. Hardy is group chief executive and global managing partner of Langdon & Matthews International Audit and Financial Services. In that call, Charles was advised that, effective immediately, he would be promoted to managing partner of Langdon & Matthews in the UK. While he felt that he had been the front-runner for this position since his old boss was promoted and transferred to Paris three months ago, it was great news and something of a relief to get the confirmation. He looked forward to celebrating his good news with his wife and family that weekend. After all, he had worked long and hard for this opportunity and it was his at last.

While the majority of the phone call was taken up with talking about Charles' promotion and Rich's promise of help and support for him in his new role, Rich also mentioned that the beginning of next quarter would also mark the date the organisational restructuring would become effective. Charles didn't have much background on this proposal – other than hearing that 'something was in the wind' from his former boss before he left for Paris – about changing from a geographic structure to a global business unit structure, whatever that meant.

Background

Langdon & Matthews, headquartered in Atlanta, USA, is a mid-size international audit and financial services firm. It has three main businesses, all of which are well represented in the UK:

- Audit Services
- Tax Advice and Planning
- Financial Systems Consulting

Langdon & Matthews generates approximately 50 per cent of its income in the US, 35 per cent in Europe and 15 per cent in Latin America.

The UK branch, based in the City of London, was acquired and developed from a local accountancy firm in 1995 and has enjoyed solid growth since then. Much of this expansion has been due to the significant growth of inward investment into the UK during this time. L&M currently employs 180 accountants, consultants and associates in the UK, including a small office of 20 people in Edinburgh. The Scottish office was established in 2000, to support a growing number of their clients who are engaged in healthcare/medical device manufacturing in Scotland.

Charles Ingham is a chartered accountant and joined L&M from its start-up in the UK in 1995. In the past, Charles has been highly rated for his audit and accountancy work and has demonstrated sound leadership qualities when warranted. He has established excellent working relationships with L&M client financial controllers in the UK. Prior to this new promotion, Charles was head of audit practice in London.

Atlanta Visit

A week after his call from Hardy, Charles travelled to Atlanta for a series of meetings, including his first meeting with Hardy's group staff. Immediately prior to his departure, he was surprised to discover that Mike Bellamy, who heads up the tax advice and planning service in London, and Joan Thornhill, who heads up the financial systems consulting services, had also been summoned to Atlanta to discuss their respective groups' budget planning processes for the coming year. That struck Charles as odd. Surely, they should be reviewing their budgets with him later, back in London? However, he acknowledged to himself that he was only just appointed so there was no point in making a big fuss about it for now. However, there was an even bigger surprise to come.

The Rich Hardy staff meeting was totally devoted to a single agenda item: a reorganisation of the business from a geographic structure to a global services product line structure. As the meeting proceeded, it slowly began to worry Charles that the new promotion he had received was possibly shaping up to be not much more than a 'shell' role and that much of the three business strategies were now going to be strategised from outside the UK. It began to be clearer now as to why Bellamy and Thornhill were in separate meetings down the hall.

That evening, Hardy invited Charles out for dinner. Over drinks and a dinner that Charles could scarcely recall later, Hardy explained some of the 'drivers' for this major organisational change:

- Stalled revenue growth over the past two years, while expenses continued to rise.
- A belief (held by Hardy and others) that a global product line structure would provide greater focus and organisational flexibility and also help to arrest the expense growth curve.
- Most importantly, multinational clients wanted to get a global financial view of their operations as opposed to the rather piecemeal country-by-country view of the past. They were also seeking much greater flexibility and adaptability from all their service providers.

From the evening conversation and from the meeting earlier in the day, it was clear to Charles that this decision was already made and that implementation was already on track in many of the countries. There was no point in trying to persuade senior management that the UK was different or that extra time was needed to implement the change. Unfortunately, the recent change of leadership in the UK had delayed any serious planning for this organisational change and his former boss had done him no favours by failing to outline these changes to him sooner.

Hardy stressed the importance of the country manager role and that the organisation needed both the business product line structure and a good country manager structure, supporting and driving the product line structure 'on the ground'. Hardy described the structure as a matrix and, while Bellamy and Thornhill would report to their product line leaders in Atlanta, they would have a 'dotted line' reporting relationship to Charles.

Back Home

On his flight back to London, Charles thought about his predicament and came up with three major concerns:

- On a personal basis, he was concerned that the job he had worked so hard for over those ten years might evolve into something of a 'shell' role and that much business development strategy was going to be done outside the UK and over his head. Was it possible that his long-sought prize of being 'L&M's king of Britain' was going to be minimised?
- Bellamy and Thornhill would now report to their respective group business leaders back in Atlanta. So what was his new role going to be? What was his relationship going to be with them? He was told that they would have a 'dotted line' reporting relationship to him but what did that mean at the end of the day? He had a good enough relationship with both Bellamy and Thornhill until now but how would those relationships fare after these changes?
- Should he go ahead and appoint his successor as head of audit services in London?

Over the weekend, Rich Hardy telephoned Charles and spent quite some time reassuring him further of the importance of his new role and the significant leadership role that was necessary 'on the ground' in the UK. Always the pragmatist, Charles came into the office on the Monday morning, having picked himself up and dusted himself off. He had begun to believe that Hardy was perhaps right; that there was real value in the role. Maybe it wasn't a smaller role after all but just a different role, requiring different skills and behaviours than in the past?

He decided to arrange a meeting with Bellamy and Thornhill for the following day to discuss all of this. Later, his secretary came back to advise that Thornhill was available for the meeting but that Bellamy was already booked on a flight back to Atlanta on Tuesday. Had the games begun?

Questions:

1. Analyse the key organisational issues facing Langdon & Matthews in the UK now and how might they be best addressed?
2. What immediate actions should Charles take and why?
3. Should Charles proceed and appoint his successor to his old position as head of audit?

CHAPTER 5

TEAM-BASED STRUCTURES

Introduction

The concept of teams clearly has its origins in sport. Applying the concept to business, teams are typically groups of employees with complimentary skills and competencies, working collaboratively towards common goals. Katzenbach and Smith (1993: 45), in their influential work on teams, define a team in a business setting as 'a small number of people with complimentary skills who are committed to a common purpose, performance goals and approach for which they hold themselves mutually accountable.' Lawler suggests that there are five important types of teams in organisations: problem-solving teams, work teams, project teams, overlay teams (coordinating and aligning the work of other groups, e.g. customer service across different business units to present one face to the customer) and management teams; 'they differ in purpose, duration and membership and each type is suited to a particular set of organisational circumstances and goals' (1996: 131).

The focus on teams in this chapter is in the context of organisation design. On that basis, we will largely ignore short-term project teams and problem-solving or quality improvement teams. Instead, the chapter will focus on work teams, which are used as a central building-block of organisation design.

The chapter will also explore the development of teams in a business setting; discuss whether teams are a strategy in their own right or an enabler of strategy implementation; consider the degree of autonomy enjoyed by teams; outline important cultural, organisational and physical requirements necessary to promote effective teams; and look at the effects of geographic and organisational cultural differences in team development.

Development of Teams in a Business Setting

Throughout the second half of the twentieth century, organisations and research groups have experimented with newer, flatter structures. The London Tavistock Institute created the concept of autonomous work groups; Scandinavian car manufacturers Saab and Volvo dramatically changed from mass-production assembly lines to small work cells where teams completed whole stages of car assembly in specially designed factory layouts. The experience of these changes in auto assembly is well-chronicled and includes improved productivity and product quality, cost reduction, considerably reduced employee turn-over, and improved industrial relations. The Tavistock research and the Scandinavian auto industry experience showed that an organisation's technical or operating systems needed to be balanced and integrated with the needs of the organisation's social systems. This led to the development of newer approaches to work, often referred to in the literature as socio-technical systems. This represented a substantial shift from the earlier teaching of Frederick W. Taylor and his scientific management approach (see Chapter 2). Given the success of these work group initiatives in terms of improved productivity, reduced turnover, and so on, it is hardly surprising that companies such as Milliken, G.E., IBM, Procter & Gamble, Best Foods, Corning, and many others have since introduced work team structures in their organisations.

However, it must be pointed out that, despite Volvo's acclaimed socio-technical approach from the late 1960s through to the early 1990s, market forces in the global automotive industry were changing throughout this time and Volvo, like others, was forced to take serious measures to respond to those changes. Though its socio-technical approach yielded positive results in terms of improved quality of cars, its productivity (thirty-two hours per vehicle) was behind the mass production lines of Japan (twenty-one hours per car) and the US (twenty-five hours per vehicle). Volvo's response included closing the Uddevalla and Kalmar factories and consolidating these operations into a larger factory at Torslanda. In 1999, Volvo sold its car business to Ford. However, despite its difficulties, Volvo has persisted with its socio-tech approach in many of its other factories, including its truck plant in Ghent, Belgium, emphasising its continued commitment to its core principles of teams and minimum hierarchy (Prashanth 2004).

Autonomous work groups, sometimes referred to as self-directed work teams, work on a variety of processes (e.g. order fulfilment) or products (e.g. yield improvement). These groups typically plan their own work, manage problems that arise, schedule their own vacations, and so on. In short, the group manages most things among themselves that a supervisor would traditionally do. These groups work on their objectives on an on-going, open-ended basis. They are not specially convened groups initiated to work on a short-term special project. These teams are basically the architectural building block by which a substantial amount of the organisation's work gets done.

The Concept of Teams as Strategy in its Own Right or as an Enabler of Strategy?

Terms such as teams and teamwork are value-laden. They are terms similar to quality, customer-service, and so on; concepts that one can scarcely argue against. However, for work teams to be successful, they must be part of a clear business strategy. I suggest that the concept of teams does not constitute a strategy in itself but rather is an enabler to achieve a strategy. Work teams can be part of an overall strategy of de-layering to create flatter, 'leaner' organisational structures. Teams are not an end in themselves and organisations need to avoid 'the fallacy of programmatic change' (Beer, Eisenstat and Spector 1990).

Some organisations measure the 'health' of teams in their organisation simply by measuring the number of active teams; they see this goal as an end in itself. Arguably, they have somehow missed the point that teams are an enabler or methodology by which work gets done and strategies executed. According to Katzenbach and Smith, 'in organisations with weak performance ethics or cultures, leaders will provide a sounder foundation for teams by addressing and demanding performance than by embracing the latest organisation design fad, including teams themselves' (1993:13).

Levels of Autonomy

Experience has shown that, for many organisations, empowering teams is an evolutionary process. It does not start by management posting a notice saying 'effective next Monday we will have empowerment.' The shift towards empowered work teams is not binary: today, close monitoring and supervision; tomorrow, empowered teams. Many would describe this shift as a journey. There is much evidence of work teams managing their own production schedules, shift rosters and vacation plans. Some teams do their own employment interviewing and make selection decisions. Some undertake budget setting and control while others assess individual team member performance and address training needs. Moving along the continuum from close supervision to empowerment, the question is regularly asked about how much decision-making discretion a team can undertake. It is hard to imagine a work team in McDonald's in the suburbs of San Diego or Moscow being permitted to change the recipe for the 'Big Mac' at their own discretion. Having said that, there is a lot that teams can decide and manage for themselves.

Acknowledging that most teams are not completely autonomous, there is often a manager or work-group leader who assumes some traditional first-level supervisory responsibilities, together with other managerial responsibilities. Managers in such organisations have very large spans of control, sometimes ranging over 100 team members. For example, AT&T Operator Services in Richmond, VA, USA, moved successfully from a span of control of one manager for twelve team members, to one manager for teams of up to seventy-two team members (Wellins *et al.* 1993).

Cultural, Organisational and Physical Requirements for Teams

There are a number of important cultural, organisational and physical requirements necessary to promote the successful development of work teams in organisations:

1. Fundamental Shift in Thinking

For many organisations there needs to be a fundamental shift in thinking at the highest levels. It is unlikely that any initiative towards work teams will be successful when all that employees observe is 'internecine warfare' at the top of the organisation.

2. New Managerial Role

As teams evolve and grow, the traditional role of the manager changes dramatically. The evolution represents a shift from the command and control model to one of less direct involvement. For many managers, being less 'hands-on' can create a feeling of being less in control and uncertain about how to find the right balance between giving help and meddling. I recall one manager saying to me that one of the hardest things he ever had to do as a manager was to let the team get on with solving an urgent problem and not dive in himself with his 'fireman's helmet and hatchet'. In team-based structures, the role of the manager is much more that of a coach and facilitator. Managers need the confidence and training to fulfil this very different skill set.

3. Selection and Training

A work team structure also requires careful team member selection. Selection is typically conducted by the line manager with HR support. There appears to be little evidence, beyond a few leading companies including Milliken, of actual team members being involved in selection methods. There is also a need for considerable investment in training. Team members need not only to be able to perform the operational tasks but also be able to operate well as a team, typically in an unsupervised environment. Successful work team environments such as Milliken, Xerox and Procter & Gamble invest significant sums in developing team skills and supporting mechanisms. See Table 5.1 for important organisational 'engineering' to support team-based structures.

4. Mutual Accountability

There is much rhetoric in prefixing the term 'high-performance' to work teams. Calling a team 'a high-performance team' doesn't of itself make it a high performer. Katzenbach and Smith report that truly high-performance teams are extremely rare (1993). They suggest that a high degree of personal commitment to one another is what differentiates high-performance teams from other teams. Their definition of teams, which was detailed at the beginning of this chapter, is important because it not only addresses the need for a combination of complimentary skills but also raises the issue of team members holding each other mutually accountable. This includes proactively addressing issues – not opting out or blaming others – flexibility, and willingness to take on tasks outside of one's own direct discipline or skill. Alexander Dumas' 'Three Musketeers' motto perhaps best captures the principle:

'All for one and one for all'. According to Katzenbach and Smith, 'At its core, team accountability is about the sincere promises we make to ourselves and to others, promises that underpin two critical aspects of teams: commitment and trust. By promising to hold ourselves accountable to the team's goals, we each earn the right to express our own views about all aspects of the team's efforts and to have our own views receive a fair and constructive hearing' (1993: 60). I believe that this issue of mutual accountability can be reduced to just two words: trust and openness.

Table 5.1: Organisational 'Engineering' to Support Team-based Organisational Structures

Factor	Team-based Work Groups	Traditional Supervising Structures
Structure	Flatter structures	Taller structures
Jobs/roles	Broader, multi-skilled roles	Narrowly defined roles
Supervisory Style	Supervisor coaches, advises, facilitates	Close supervision Supervisor schedules work
Hiring/ selection	Team selects	HR or supervisor selects
Training	Extensive and expensive training	Minimum training
Pay	Competency-based pay plus team bonus	Individual pay or union rate
Information flow	Extensive flows, both directions	Minimal flow
Decision making	Team decision making on many matters	Hierarchical decision making

5. Meeting Space

A team structure also requires sufficient meeting space accommodation or facilities layout to allow teams to meet regularly as part of their work. Meeting rooms or space to meet on the factory floor or administrative office open-plan area often seem to be over-demanded and under-supplied. Space can encourage or inhibit information and dialogue exchange.

Latent Capacity to Accommodate Exceptional Growth?

Theory & Practice

While there are significant advantages in a work team structure as outlined above, a very flat team structure may not have the organisational 'fat', latent capacity, or requisite redundancy to manage exceptional growth and keep to its original design. The explosive workforce growth experienced by a Motorola Scottish manufacturing facility illustrates the point. In 1991, Motorola set up a 'greenfield' telecoms manufacturing facility in Easter Inch in east Scotland. The organisational structure was designed to have only three layers of management with work teams established across the organisation. The layers were site leader (general manager), functional leader (director) and a team leader (manager). The latter role initially rotated between all team members on a one- to three-month basis before settling on the best leader as viewed by the team. In this very flat structure all employees were called 'associates' and there were no internal job descriptions beyond functional areas, e.g. manufacturing associate, finance associate, and so on. Work areas were very egalitarian with open-plan layouts across the production areas. As one might imagine, this structure was very effective for information flow, dramatically reducing lead times for decisions, and creating greater 'ownership' among team members during this critical start-up period. The workforce increased from zero to 500 employees in the first 12 months of operation and doubled to 1000 in the following 12 months. Former employees report that the original structure seemed to function well up to a capacity of about 700 employees. However, when the staff numbers went above that, cracks began to appear in the structure as the sheer spans of control were becoming unmanageable. To address these problems, an extra layer was added: line/process lead (supervisor).

By the time the workforce reached 1,500, the spans of control had continued to crack and the company added further and perhaps more traditional supervision for evening and nightshifts.

> *This additional traditional supervisory layer was also added because of the growing use of third-party contract employees as Motorola sought to be able to flex manufacturing costs and workforce levels to product demand cycles. Having peaked at over 2,000 associates, the facility finally succumbed to much lower Asian production costs and closed operations in 2002. By that stage it had reverted to a more 'traditional' five-layer, tall organisational structure.*

Geographic and Organisational Cultural Differences

The research of Hofstede (1980), and Trompenaars and Hampden-Turner (1998) on geographic cultural differences suggest that team involvement may be more compatible with some cultures than with others. These authors indicate that in countries with high power distance (cultures where there is a rigid social hierarchy and employees are more comfortable when supervisors give them direct instructions), employees are much less likely to be comfortable in a team that has a lot of discretion in decision making. This research, supported by Katzenbach and Smith (1993), also suggests that strong individualistic cultures may be less comfortable with team involvement because of their preference to work on an individual basis. McShane and Von Ginlow report that 'Mexico has a very high power distance value system, which explains why firms have difficulty implementing self-directed work teams in that country' (2003: 281).

On a cautionary note, we should be careful about leaping to conclusions and making some sweeping generalisations about different cultures. What the research of Hofstede, Trompenaars and Hampton-Turner does is to alert organisations to the need for geographic cultural sensitivity and to warn of the dangers of applying management practices or structures without the necessary adaptation to different countries and cultures; one approach doesn't work in every situation, and one size doesn't fit all. Few geographic cultures are so extreme in either power distance, individualism or other differences, however, that they rule out involvement and engagement in teams. The research should help organisations to better plan and tailor their training for the different countries and cultures in which they operate.

Difficulties arising from cultural variations in different countries can be amplified when a team is made up of members from different geographic regions and cultures. In addition to working in substantially different time zones, other challenges to such teams might include differing styles of communication (direct versus indirect), accents and fluency, differing attitudes towards hierarchy and authority, and conflicting norms in decision making. The good news, however, is that intra-team cultural variations are manageable if managers and team members avoid imposing single-culture-based assumptions and approaches on multicultural situations (Brett, Behfar and Kern 2006).

Similar to the issues of differences in geographic culture are organisational cultural differences that could undermine team development. In the 1980s, Apple placed high value on individual creativity, which had served them well through their early development phase. However, the continuing growth of the company required much greater collaboration across key departments and they established cross-functional teams. Because of the deeply rooted culture of individualism, these teams of R&D, marketing and manufacturing personnel failed to achieve the necessary collaboration (Griffith 1997).

HR reward processes, including pay and promotion, are also likely to have a profound effect on aiding or retarding effective teamwork. Individual performance appraisal ratings and rankings, with consequential effects on personal pay increases and promotion opportunities, can easily create an environment of competition among and between team members. Such intra-team competition and rivalry is unlikely to foster an environment where collaboration, information-sharing and mutual accountability are the norm.

Conclusion

To conclude, work teams represent a substantial and radical departure from traditional scientific management and conventional organisational structures. While they are most frequently found in manufacturing environments, the concept is just as relevant in any setting where people work interdependently and interactively and can be collectively responsible for designing a product, making a product or providing an administrative service. A study of sixty-three matched pairs of traditionally managed groups and self-managed teams doing similar work in one telephone company found that the self-managed teams were rated higher in productivity, quality, customer service and safety. The study also found that the self-managed teams enjoyed higher levels of job satisfaction, social satisfaction and trust than the traditionally managed groups (Cohen 1993). However, the challenges to creating an effective team-based structure must not be underestimated. Key among these challenges is visible top management commitment, a substantial investment in training for both multi-skills and team behaviours, team-based rewards and training for managers in their evolving new roles. As in the case of Motorola's experience, work teams may not be sufficiently robust to cope with extraordinarily rapid growth.

The development and evolution of work teams has been described as a journey. Given that teams may not have complete discretion in decision making, it may be that it is a journey without an eventual destination, but one perhaps still worth the travails of travel.

Case Based on Chapter 5

Jack Strauss, bar and restaurant manager at the Hampton Indian Island Spa and Golf Resort, was undecided about what to do. His bar staff did not seem to be working well as a team, as he had hoped they would. He could see that relationships amongst some team members were a little strained and his concern was that the strain was beginning to show through poorer customer service, especially at the very busy times before dinner and again later in the evening.

Background

The Hampton Indian Island Resort is a 4-star hotel, spa and golf resort, located in the Hamptons, on the east side of Long Island, New York, USA. The Hamptons is a well-known summer retreat for the rich and well-to-do of New York. The hospitality industry in the area tends to be very seasonal with very high occupancy rates from June to Labour Day in September and very little business for the rest of the year. As a consequence, much of the hotel's work is temporary summer work, and it typically employs college students (aged twenty-one and above) for bar work. This situation is ideal for college students and hotel management alike as the demand for staff corresponds directly with

64

college vacations. Students like working in the Hamptons as there are many attractions locally during their time off and hotel clientele tend to be good tippers. These temporary employees live and eat at the hotel employee dormitory at the rear of the hotel. Pay rates are low but 'room and board' is free and tips are excellent. Summer employees come from upstate New York and from as far away as Ireland and the UK, working on student visas.

The hotel has three large, busy bars: the main bar ('Ricks'), a pool-side bar ('Sandals') and a bar at the golf clubhouse ('the 19th'). During high season, Strauss needs two bar staff to cover 11.00 a.m. to 8.00 p.m. at the pool-side and two staff at the golf clubhouse for the same hours; two bar staff from 11.00 a.m. to 7.00 p.m. in the main bar and three staff there from 7.00 p.m. to 1.00 a.m. approximately. Allowing for these shifts and scheduled days off, Strauss has a team of ten bar personnel: five men and five women. Some of these shifts are busier than others and, in the interest of fairness, the ten people cover all shifts and locations over a monthly roster.

The Situation

Strauss had worked as bar and restaurant manager with the hotel chain for the previous five years, spending the summers in the Hamptons and the winters in a sister hotel in Aspen. Two years ago, senior hotel management decided to keep the management structure very flat and use work teams wherever possible to manage their own departmental activities. Since then, Strauss has managed the bar staff as a team and the restaurant staff as another team. He encouraged the bar team to agree among themselves how and when they stocked shelves from central stores; how they managed their work schedules between them; and how they shared tips. Of the ten people he hired this summer for the bars, only two had worked in the hotel before. The other eight were new to the hotel and to the area. Given that the bars were so busy so early in the season, he has had very little time with the group together and most of his communication was to whoever was on duty at the time, expecting them to pass on the information to the others at shift change.

Joe Roccio was a senior at a state college in up-state New York and had started his first summer at the hotel. He had heard great things about the Hamptons and this hotel, and so far he wasn't disappointed. There was, however, one thing that did bother Joe. Because his boss, Jack Strauss, had largely delegated the management of the bars to the team, the two people that had worked there before were beginning to assert themselves and boss him and the others around as if they were joint supervisors. In addition to their inclination to boss everyone around, they had also become quite tardy at shift change-over themselves. Just two nights ago, Joe had to stay on for three quarters of an hour after scheduled shift change because one of these two was late for work and, as a consequence, Joe ended up being late for what was to have been a special date. As Joe rushed away he expressed his annoyance in a frank and forthright manner. Since then, Joe and his colleague have not spoken to each other.

Jack Strauss continues to be undecided about what to do with the team and the current climate. He wants the team to behave like the autonomous work teams he read about and was concerned that any intervention on his part might undermine the concept of an autonomous team. He was also very busy as the hotel was booked solid for the next four weeks.

Questions

1. What are the key group dynamics at work in this situation?
2. What should Jack Strauss do and why?
3. What should Joe Roccio do and why?

CHAPTER 6

HYBRID AND OTHER STRUCTURES

Introduction

While earlier chapters discussed specific structures, e.g. functional, geographic, and so on, the reality for many organisations is that they have hybrids of many of these structures. Matrix structures, discussed in Chapter 4, are indeed hybrids in their own right. The purpose of this chapter is to explore some of these composite arrangements. Such structures include front/back structures, project team structures, networked organisations (intercompany and intracompany), and communities of practice.

Front/Back Structures

A front/back structure is a composite structure whereby the organisation is part structured around customers and markets (the front-end of the business) and part structured around internal processes such as developing brands, manufacturing or administrative processes in financial services (the back-end of the business). The logic of this structure is to achieve closeness to the customer on the one hand, while at the same time achieving economies of scale and avoiding duplicated cost. An example of a front/back structure could be where an organisation is structured around strategic business units (SBUs) and is focused on key markets, while all manufacturing is centralised in order to achieve economies of scale, functional excellence and leverage with third party subcontractors. In his highly influential work on organisation design, Galbraith (2002) cites Boeing's commercial aircraft division as a front/back structure. It is structured around business units selling narrow-bodied planes (e.g. 737 and 757) and wide-bodied planes (747 and 767). However, the facilities and equipment cost of fabrication and assembly of aircraft is so extraordinarily expensive that they cannot be duplicated in each business unit. In this case there is a hybrid structure of strategic business units and functions: business units dealing with markets and customers, with manufacturing costs centralised and shared between the businesses.

Theory & Practice

Galbraith (2002) refers to Procter & Gamble (P&G) as an example of a front/back structure.

P&G is organised by global business units (GBUs) (e.g. fabric and home care, beauty products, and so on), that market and manufacture their products around the world. GBUs are responsible for building brands and spreading product innovations across the company's product categories and geographic markets. In addition to GBUs based on product lines, P&G has market development organisations (MDOs), which are organised by geography. P&G's experience is that the geographically based MDOs move strategic initiatives to markets faster, more creatively, and at less cost. The MDOs tailor the company's global programmes to local markets and use their knowledge of local consumers and retailers to guide the entire business (Procter & Gamble: 2007).

In the five years up to 2006, P&G achieved compound sales growth of 12 per cent per annum and 24 per cent per annum earnings growth. In 2006 it was listed in Fortune *magazine's Top Most Profitable Companies,* Forbes' *America's top 500 companies, and* Business Week *showed it at number 6 in the World's 25 Most Innovative Companies. That same year it won, among other international awards, the UK Customer Service Award and Fortune 500 Most Influential Multinational Companies in China.*

It seems evident from P&G's continually impressive global business results and recognition awards that their front/back structures operate very effectively indeed.

In exploring P&G's structures, one cannot but be impressed that their organisation designs are dynamic; continuously adjusting to its ever-changing environments externally (e.g. markets) and internally (e.g. acquisitions). This commitment to continuous adjustment of organisation design would appear to be one of the forces that separate it from other companies.

Project Team Structures

There is a type of project team structure, where individuals with different but complimentary skills are brought together for a specific business assignment, typically for the term of the project. It is possible, even likely, that individual team participants will change from one project, business deal or operation to the next. A film or television studio is likely to mix and match directors, film crews and set design personnel for a particular project and then reassign them to other projects once the film is 'in the can'. A multi-disciplined surgical team is another example of an operation or project based structure. In this example, individuals have highly complimentary skills and are matched together depending on the type of surgery and availability of particular individuals. Some organisations establish project teams around deal opportunities. In order to pursue a particular deal opportunity, some organisations set up a team of specialists depending on the type of deal, location and availability of individuals. Once the deal is completed, the organisation may reassign individual team members to other teams, depending on the next business opportunities.

Theory & Practice
GE Capital Aviation Services (GECAS), which leases aircraft to airlines, is organised around regional 'deal teams'. These teams are comprised of marketing people and underwriters, along with financial, service and operations people for a particular customer or deal, and then reform as necessary for the next business opportunity (Ashkenas et al. 2002).

Shared Services

Some organisations have reduced costs and increased flexibility by combining parts of different departments, for example finance and

HR, that have similar and complimentary capabilities. It is not that long ago that finance and HR prepared separate workforce numbers at the end of each month, and spent a good portion of the following month reconciling their differing numbers!

Organisations are also establishing shared service arrangements on a geographic basis. Companies with operations across many EU countries do not necessarily need payroll, HR administration and accounts payable functions in each of the countries. Increasingly, organisations are combining national administrative functions into regional centres to achieve economies of scale and lower administrative costs.

Networked Organisations: Intercompany

Focusing on their core competencies, some companies restrict their operations to those few capabilities that are the essential heart of their business, and let outside specialists and experts manage everything else (Handy 1990; Daft 2001). Long gone are the days when companies employed their own cafeteria staff, security guards and cleaners.

Theory & Practice

Today, most US semiconductor companies subcontract the back-end of their manufacturing processes to specialist assembly and test subcontractors in the Philippines (e.g. Amkor), Singapore (e.g. STATS), and China (e.g. ASAT). Other semiconductor companies Cirrus Logic and Xilinx are even subcontracting the much higher value-added front-end wafer fabrication activities. These newer 'fabless' semiconductor companies focus on their critical core competencies of marketing and product design and rely on such wafer fabrication foundries as Taiwan Semiconductor Manufacturing Company (TSMC) for their intricate front-end manufacturing processes. The advantages of subcontracting these activities include the following:

- *Because of their considerable scale of operations and low labour cost locations, subcontractors can provide substantially lower manufacturing cost solutions; and*

> • *because of scale and lower costs, these subcontractors can afford to invest in semiconductor manufacturing technologies much more than any one of their customers can and they offer these newer engineering capabilities to their customers.*

In 2003, Procter & Gamble and Hewlett Packard signed a ten-year $3 billion contract under which HP Services would manage P&G's IT infrastructure, data centre operations, desktop and end user support, network management, applications development and maintenance across 160 countries.

The networked organisation might best be depicted as a central hub surrounded by an array of outside subcontractors and other service providers (see Figure 6.1).

Figure 6.1: The Networked Organisation

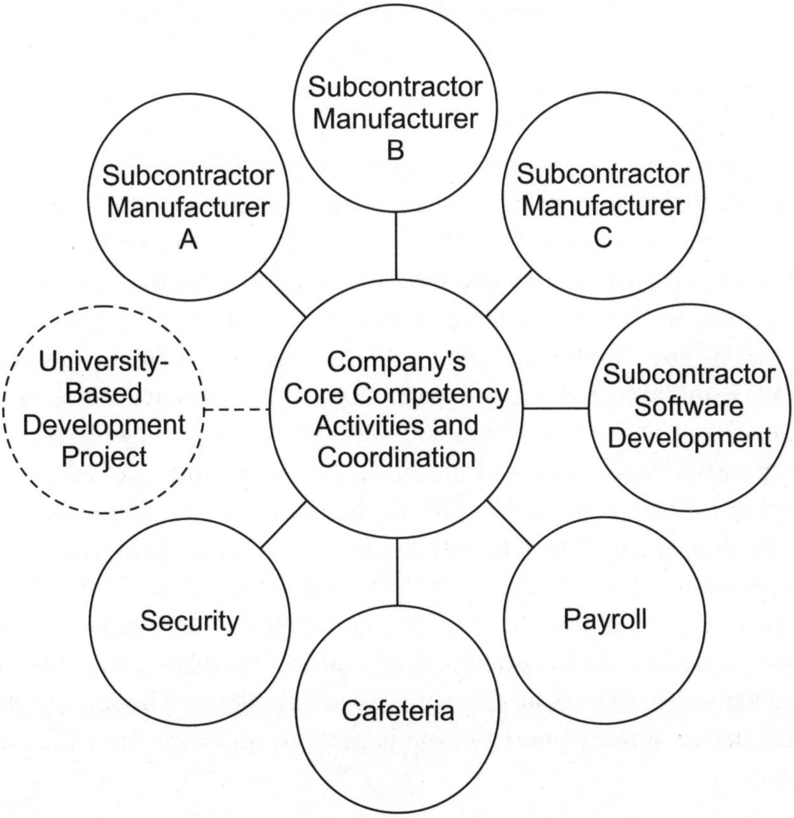

Similar to an organisation that is over-reliant on a single customer, an organisation that is over-reliant on a single source of supply is hugely exposed. Well-managed companies will have a few reliable suppliers and will actively manage these relationships as longer-term strategic alliances. In order to manage those alliances, companies need to acquire and develop supply chain skills including relationship management, supplier quality audit processes, and so on.

Increasingly, companies are electronically connected to their subcontractors' production control systems. When a customer orders a router from Cisco on their website, the order is automatically downloaded to Flextronics Ltd., a contract manufacturer in California. Flextronics then ship the product directly to the customer, without Cisco employees ever touching the part (Daft 2001). Dell is a good example of a company networked, in the first instance, to their customers (who order online) to their factory locations and their assembly sub-contractors, to Microsoft (whose software they load), and to their shipping contractors. While naturally described as an IT company, with state-of-the-art products, Dell might also be described as a highly networked logistics company.

Amazon.com is another good example of a highly networked, almost virtual company. After losing more than $2 billion in its first six years in business, Amazon has spent the last five years streamlining operations, adding everything from beauty products to gardening tools to its on-line virtual store and building a network of over one million merchants and individual sellers through its systems.

Child and Faulkner (1998) distinguish between a dominated network and an equal partner network. In the dominated network, the organisation at the hub dominates and practically controls some of the network suppliers by virtue of its size and influence. Marks and Spencer in the UK and Wal-Mart in the US have so much negotiation leverage, they can almost dictate to their suppliers what to make, when to make it, to deliver it just in time (JIT) and how much to charge for it. At the other end of the spectrum, the equal partner arrangement can be characterised by small collections of companies, who share a high co-dependency for their mutual benefit and development. The collaborative effort between Sony and Ericsson is perhaps an example of the equal partner arrangement. The stated reason for this collaboration was to leverage Sony's consumer electronics and digital camera expertise with Ericsson's technological leadership in the telecommunications sector. Both companies have now ceased making their own brands of mobile phones and only sell the collaborative product. Other examples of equal partner arrangements may be found in computing and biotechnology firms in Silicon Valley in California, Route 128 in Massachusetts, and other technology development locations.

Child and Faulkner (1998) do make the point that supplier and subcontractor relationships have been around for a very long time with their own detailed contracts and relationships, without being referred to as networks. What is different about some of these relationships today is their nature, characterised by the electronic interconnectivity and sharing of information and forecasts, and the sense of real partnership and collaboration. They are managed more as longer-term strategic alliances.

Advantages of inter-company networks include:

- Adaptability: networks are more flexible and fluid than traditional organisations. As a consequence, networked organisations can respond more quickly to changes in the marketplace.
- Companies can focus on their core competencies and contract out activities that other organisations can do better and/or more cheaply than they can.
- Because of their huge scale of operations and usually low labour-cost locations, subcontractors can provide low-cost manufacturing and service solutions that their clients could never match.
- Again, because of scale and lower costs, these subcontractors can afford to invest in their offered technologies much more than any one of their clients can and they offer these newer engineering capabilities to their clients.
- Companies do not have to worry about adjusting their workforce to meet peaks and troughs in demand. Subcontractors may be able to aggregate client demands by offsetting the peak of one client with the trough of another.

- Information technology allows client companies to manage their networks as quickly as if the service was internal to their own operations.

Disadvantages of a networked organisation include:

- Outsourcing a core competency, meaning essentially giving the 'crown jewels' to a subcontractor, who may subsequently use that competency and compete against the client, or offer that competency to a competitor.
- Outsourcing a core competency to a subcontractor who may not be able to achieve the same quality standards. Toyota retains in-house processes such as stamping, welding and injection moulding that give them control over the fit and finish of their cars, even though some of these processes could be undertaken elsewhere at a lower price (Child 2005).
- Being over-reliant on a single supplier. An organisation that is over-reliant on a single source of supply is hugely exposed. Many companies have a few suppliers and, while this spread of business may reduce their negotiation leverage with any one subcontractor, they feel that the trade-off of price leverage in favour of multiple sources is worth it.

Networked Organisations: Intracompany

In Chapter 3 we noted that SBUs can become silos of knowledge and expertise, not open or accessible to members of other business units, and that critical core competencies can be fragmented across sub-optimised units. Key performance indicators and pay/reward structures, which are based solely on SBU performance, may also have the effect of creating significant competition between the units, which in turn is unlikely to lead to greater sharing of information and best practice (see case study in Chapter 8).

Communities of Practice

In order to reduce competition and silo mentality and manage knowledge more effectively, some organisations have promoted and fostered cross-unit forums and communities of practice.

Communities of practice are informal groups of people with a shared interest/practice area who come together to collaborate over an extended period to share ideas and develop innovative solutions to issues in their common interest area. Membership of a community of practice is based on interest and knowledge, so membership tends to span organisational structures and boundaries – members can operate across and even between organisations. They vary in areas of interest, size of group, formality of engagement, but they are all characterised by members' willingness to share their experiences and knowledge in an open and creative way, unencumbered by hierarchy and organisational politics.

Communities of practice are 'not a new kind of organisational unit; rather they are a different cut on the organisation's structure – one that emphasises the learning that people have done together rather than the unit they report to, the project they are working on, or the people they know' (Wenger 1998: 2). The communities of practice model has attracted attention in organisation studies in the context of increasing emphasis on knowledge as a key organisational asset. The informal, organic and open nature of communities of practice is seen as an important concept for creating and sharing new organisational knowledge that informs the work of members in their regular organisational units, departments, teams and networks.

Communities of practice are often self-organising systems that may be difficult to reconcile with traditional organisational hierarchies. Some communities of practice survive quite well without any attention from the formal organisation, and would in fact prefer to operate 'under the radar'. However, most would benefit from some facilitation on the part of the formal organisation in terms of time allowed for community activities, recognition, resources, and so on. The formal organisation needs to learn the 'art of balancing design and emergence' (Wenger 1998: 2) by weaving a delicate path between supporting communities of practice without compromising their essential self-organising and spontaneous nature.

These informal communities of practice can be as informal as a gathering at a coffee break, with much use of backs of napkins, 'brown bag lunches' (where functional specialists may give a somewhat more formal presentation on their current work interest over lunch break), and more formal internal conferences. Such networks encourage people with common interests to collaborate proactively and openly and not be encumbered by hierarchy, or departmental politics, real or imagined.

Case Based on Chapter 6

David Clark wasn't sleeping well at night. His bookselling business was slowing down in recent years and while he continued to add stores across the US, his sales growth per store continued to slow. Online book sales, especially by Amazon.com, were rapidly taking a significant and growing market share.

Background

David and his two younger brothers owned a large chain of book stores across the US: Clarks Bookstores. The business was founded by their parents, Joshua and Catherine, in the mid-1950s in the San Francisco area. David and his brothers took over the business in the early 1980s and refurbished the old stores and built new ones with a focus on creating a unique book browsing and buying experience for customers.

The new large and bright stores, often co-located with large and fashionable shopping malls, pushed many small and independent booksellers out of business, especially in the larger urban areas. In addition to vast displays of books, there were areas with comfortable chairs where prospective buyers could thumb through books at their leisure; all their newer stores had coffee corners, where they rented space to popular coffee companies; and they also had small, supervised crèches, to allow parents to browse in comfort and at their leisure. With this recipe, it was not surprising that the stores flourished and grew in popularity west of the Rockie Mountains, throughout the 1980s and 1990s.

Apart from competitor Barnes & Noble, the other real competitive threat to Clarks Bookstores arrived in the mid-1990s in the form of the Internet. Upstart retailer Amazon.com was the very antithesis of Clarks' shopping experience, since it didn't offer comfortable stores with pleasantly wafting aromas of coffee. Instead, through Amazon.

com, customers could now just browse and buy online 24/7 from their homes or offices. What a threat Amazon turned out to be! In 2006, Amazon's revenues were $10.7 billion, 45 per cent coming from international sales and a 12 million square feet order fulfillment warehousing network.

The Situation

The Clark brothers believed that they still had the 'lion's share' of traditional over-the-counter business in the region and that there would always be a market for such sales. However, they felt that where people knew exactly what book they wanted or where a business wished to buy quantities of a publication, they were as likely to order online with Amazon. The brothers understood that they really had to seriously consider e-commerce themselves to protect and grow their market share.

Clarks Bookstores' subsequent entry into e-commerce was not successful. They made costly errors in starting out on their own in what was and is a very different business model, with different operating assumptions. Facing up to these costly errors, David Clark, as CEO, now has some serious thinking to do and tough decisions to make.

Questions

1. Consider whether or not you think Clarks should continue to pursue an e-commerce strategy. Explain your answer.
2. If Clarks should pursue an e-commerce strategy, what options are available to them to build a web-based business?
3. Which option would you select and why?
4. How would your selected option be structured and why?

CHAPTER 7

MERGERS AND ACQUISITIONS

Introduction

Mergers and acquisitions (M&As) are corporate practices of buying, or merging with, other businesses in order to achieve greater growth and synergies. M&As are about acquiring assets, businesses (e.g. brands), and/or technical knowledge to achieve expansion that is beyond normal organic growth. The theory of M&As is one of increasing scale and creating synergy so that the combination of the two organisations can produce significant strategic advantage through some or all of the following: greater scale, wider markets and geographies, and skills and technological know-how.

In an acquisition, the purchasing organisation buys the shares and control of the target company. In the case of a merger, two companies combine together into a larger organisation. A Cisco Systems acquisition of a small company with emergent technology is a clear example of an acquisition, whereas the combination of JP Morgan and Chase Manhattan has been described as a 'merger of equals'. Sometimes, however, the line between merger and acquisition becomes blurred, particularly when what is in reality an acquisition is described as a merger for political or marketing reasons.

One of the major effects of globalisation is the extraordinary growth in mergers and acquisitions over the past thirty years or so. The total world value of mergers and acquisitions was reported as topping $2.7 trillion in 2005, a 30 per cent increase over the previous year. Based on current levels of deal-making, that figure was expected to increase again in 2006 (Ettenson and Knowles 2006). However, despite the vast sums changing hands, many of these transactions have not been successful. Porter (1987) estimated that at least half of all mergers and acquisitions failed to increase shareholder value. Marks and Mirvis suggest that as many as three-quarters of corporate combinations fail to achieve their aggregate business goals:

> Most produce higher-than-expected costs and lower-than-acceptable returns. Meanwhile, executive time and operating capital are diverted from internal growth; morale, productivity and quality often plummet; talented crew members jump ship; and customers go elsewhere. (1998: 3)

Epstein (2005) and Bower (2001) draw useful distinctions between different forms of M&As. One size does not fit all. The thousands of deals that academics, consultants and business journalists lump together as mergers and acquisitions actually represent very different strategic activities, each with its own unique set of challenges. If the strategic intent is to consolidate in an industry with excess capacity, the challenge will be to determine what to rationalise and to do it quickly. On the other hand, if the strategic intent is to acquire an emerging technology, the challenge will be to hold onto the acquisition's best technologists. Bower (2001) distinguishes different types of M&A strategies, including:

- Consolidation due to excess capacity in the industry. This tends to happen in older capital-intensive industries such as automotive, steel and petrochemicals.
- Geographic expansions, which, as its name suggests, tends to occur where companies are seeking to expand into new markets. Examples include the professional services companies such as accounting and actuarial practices. The acquiring company gains access to new geographies and local management. The 'acquiree' gets access to international clients they would never achieve on their own.
- Product/market extensions are concluded in order to broaden a company's product line and international reach. Unilever's acquisition of Ben & Jerry's is an example of a product and market extension. The more recent acquisition of Gillette by Procter & Gamble is another example of product/market extension. While P&G has a strong presence in China and

Japan, Gillette has a solid foothold in countries such as India and Brazil.

- M&As as an R&D activity: some companies acquire young start-up companies, which have developed emerging new products and/or technologies, to compliment their own R&D efforts. Cisco is perhaps one of the most famous companies for acquiring small technology companies to supplement its own product/technology pipeline.

Difficulties in acquisitions can arise from unclear business strategies; lack of a comprehensive due diligence process that explores well beyond the financials; lack of an integration strategy; rampant political games and 'turf wars'; and structural problems associated with combining different functions, geographies, business units and activities. These organisational issues can be significant contributors to the ultimate success or failure of an acquisition.

How does a Ben & Jerry's ice-cream company with its young, unique and somewhat quirky background and culture become part of Unilever's, a UK-headquartered, multinational company? How do P&G and Gillette go about managing their $57 billion acquisition announced in 2005? This chapter explores the organisational issues in acquisitions and mergers; considers the reasons so many fail; and presents examples of good practice in structuring organisations for effective integration.

The Process of Mergers and Acquisitions

There are at least four broad phases in the process of M&As. These phases can be loosely described as: strategic planning and target selection; the due diligence process; pre-integration planning; and post-announcement integration and change management. These phases will be explored over the following pages (see Figure 7.1).

Phase 1: Strategic Planning and Target Selection

Some organisations do not consider sufficiently the essential strategic linkage of their business with the business being considered for acquisition or merger. Chief executives in cash-rich companies showing limited or stagnant organic growth may be put under pressure

Figure 7.1: Phases in a Mergers and Acquisitions Process

Phase 1	Phase 2	Phase 3	Phase 4
Strategic Intent	Due Diligence	Pre-Integration Planning	Post-Announcement Integration and Change Management
Clear objectives	Financial technology	Corporate branding	Well-choreographed employee meetings
Strategic fit	Sales	Short-term roles, responsibilities and CSFs	Customer visits and briefings
	Supply chain		
	Culture and climate	Decisions on structures	Supply chain integration continues
	Key personnel		
		Supply chain integration; IT integration; Employee integration, inc. laws	IT integration continues
		Communication preparation	

Deal Structure and Negotiations

by shareholders and/or the business press to 'buy' growth through acquisition. Sometimes this pressure results in a rush into action, without the necessary careful consideration of strategic fit. Sometimes an aggressive acquisition by an industry leader leads 'follower' competitors into a flurry of 'me too' initiatives, without necessarily applying the strategic pre-deal due diligence of the leader.

Companies consolidate through both vertical and horizontal integration. In the case of pharmaceutical companies, vertical integration represents an attempt to move closer to patients by acquiring major drug buyers such as health maintenance organisations (HMOs) and other large healthcare networks. On the other hand, horizontal integration of healthcare companies could represent a strategic move to gain access to newer markets, achieve greater economies of scale, or gain access to new technology or products, or, indeed, all of the above.

Theory & Practice

Upjohn was a mid-size US pharmaceutical company in a marketplace characterised by large-scale operators and small innovative companies. Upjohn could lay claim to being neither a large-scale operator nor small and innovative. It had lost patent protection on some key products, was considered weak in international sales and had a poor new product development pipeline. In 1995, Upjohn and Pharmacia A.B., a large Swedish pharmaceutical company, merged with the goals to create greater scale and to leverage their respective geographic sales reach. Pharmacia, while without any 'blockbuster' drugs, was a market leader in several product niches. Over 60 per cent of Pharmacia's sales were in Europe.

In 1995, the new company, Pharmacia & Upjohn Inc., was ranked just inside the top ten in an industry dominated by large buyers, often government departments, looking to deal with fewer suppliers.

As if to demonstrate the on-going turbulence of mergers and acquisitions, Pharmacia and Upjohn Inc. subsequently merged with Monsanto, resulting in the conglomerate Pharmacia Corp. Later it spun off its agricultural chemical division back under the name Monsanto and was itself finally acquired by Pfizer in 2003. (Weber: 1997)

Sometimes the logic of a particular acquisition seems sound, but the acquiring company only finds out after the fact that the assumptions behind the decision were flawed. Marks and Mirvis (1998) cite the example of Kodak, who wanted to become a major player in ethical drugs. Its life science division had developed good patentable products. However, obtaining regulatory approval would be difficult and marketing the new products expensive and risky. As a consequence, Kodak acquired Sterling Drug in 1988, reportedly at a premium, with a view to successfully combining Kodak's science with Sterling's regulatory management and marketing skills. As it turned out, the Sterling regulatory and marketing 'engine' proved modest enough and

Kodak divested itself of Sterling after five short years. Similarly, in 1991, AT&T acquired NCR for $8 billion because of what it saw as a convergence of computing and telecoms. Unfortunately for AT&T, customers continued to want to buy computers from computer companies, not from a telecoms carrier that rebadged computers. NCR was refloated as a stand-alone business three years later for $4 billion (Howson 2003).

The strategic vision for the combined organisation should define a rationale that identifies clear competitive advantage. That vision should be carefully considered to ensure real strategic fit between and among the parts in terms of sales reach, brand management and customer service, and, internally, in terms of people, organisational culture and potential supply chain integration/rationalisation.

Theory & Practice

The Procter & Gamble $57 billion acquisition of Gillette looks set to achieve significant strategic fit, as evidenced by the following:

- *With only a few product overlaps in deodorants and oral care, the combined organisation will now have 21 one-billion dollar brands.*
- *A P&G competency in chemistry (e.g. detergents) is complemented by Gillette's core competency in devices (razers, batteries, Braun products).*
- *P&G's focus on end-user consumers is complimented by Gillette's recognised attention to retailers.*
- *While P&G have a renowned core competency in brand management in general, and in a predominantly female marketplace in particular, Gillette's core customer segment is men. The two companies compliment their respective gender segments through the integration.*
- *The combined companies expected to save well in excess of $12 billion through rationalisation and sharing supply chain capacity.*
- *As mentioned previously, the combined organisation will be able to greatly enhance its geographic product reach*

> *into emerging high-growth geographies: Gillette in India and Brazil; P&G in China and Japan.*
>
> *In terms of results so far, P&G's Chairman and CEO A.G. Lafley, commenting on the Gillette integration, stated:*
>
> - *'We made excellent progress on the integration of Gillette. This was the largest acquisition and most complex in the consumer products industry and in P&G's history – and we're about a year ahead of schedule.'*
> - *'We expect cost synergies to be at the top end of the $1 billion to $1.2 billion target range and revenue synergies to be on target at about $750 million next fiscal year.'*
> - *'We've added 50,000 new product codes and 100,000 new shipping points to P&G systems. This enables us to go to the market as one company and to fully leverage P&G scale.'*
> - *'Our employee survey results indicate that Gillette employees are positive about their integration with P&G.'*
>
> *(P&G Annual Report 2007)*
>
> *In terms of successful M&A integration, these multi-faceted results speak for themselves.*

Phase 2: Due Diligence

Due diligence refers to the process of careful examination by the prospective acquirer of the assets, liabilities, incomes and expenditures, technologies and manufacturing processes of the company being considered for acquisition or merger. It also includes an examination in respect of potential liabilities, e.g. environmental damage liability. Other areas for examination might include employment contracts and trade union agreements.

Too often, however, acquirers confine their examination to the 'hard' dimensions of the prospective purchase, e.g. the financial, commercial and operational numbers (earnings per share (EPS), cost structures, marketshare, and so on). For successful integration to happen, prospective acquirers also need to carefully examine the 'soft' dimensions of the possible purchase, including the possibility of a clash of organisational culture between the two companies, employee competencies and capacity. The worst consequence of not examining the people dimension is the significant loss of talent right after the deal is announced, especially when the purpose of the acquisition was to acquire that talent in the first place!

A clash of organisational cultures has often been cited as a major difficulty in effecting successful M&As. Organisational culture is a concept that describes the essence or personality of an organisation. It is the set of values and guiding beliefs, often at the sub-conscious level, that underpin behaviours and decision making in an organisation. It includes not only the observable symbolism, behaviours and physical settings but, as importantly, includes the underlying values and attitudes that greatly influence 'the way things are done around here.' Cultural differences can arise in almost any dimension of corporate life, from different attitudes to customer service or approaches to quality or people management, down to something as seemingly innocuous as punctuality in starting meetings. The difficulty is that cultural attitudes are not easily recognised or measured and, as a consequence, can be somewhat taken for granted. For example, someone in an engineering company might think, 'we're all engineers here, so there should be no clash of cultures.' Research by the Sorbonne, on behalf of Hay Management Consultants, on European M&As (2004–2006) found 'culture shock' to be prevalent:

> Companies are prioritising financial and systems due diligence at the expense of the vital, intangible assets critical to a merger process, such as business culture, human capital, company structure and corporate governance. ... 58% of those surveyed confess that over-prioritising systems integration resulted in insufficient focus on intangible assets and cultural integration (http://www.peoplemanagement.co.uk).

The problem is that when change comes in direct conflict with culture, culture usually wins because it is so deeply embedded in the organisation. Differences in organisational culture should not necessarily prohibit mergers or acquisitions. What the examination of cultural differences does highlight is the need to understand the extent of differences, and the nature and degree of change management processes necessary to be put in place to address these differences.

The value in identifying these 'softer' issues and addressing them early in the integration process is highlighted in a Bain & Company survey of forty recent mergers and acquisitions. This research compared people-related practices in successful and unsuccessful deals. In fifteen deals classified as successful, nearly 90 per cent of the acquirers had identified key employees and targeted them for retention. By comparison, this task was carried out only in 30 per cent of the unsuccessful cases (Harding and Rouse 2007).

Soft due diligence takes longer to complete and is much less precise than the hard financial and operational numbers, and not every chief executive or chief financial officer either values or has the patience to wait for such exploration once the excitement of the potential acquisition is aroused. Organisational defensive routines (Argyris 1990) may also come into play whereby more junior due diligence team members, aware of the excitement and possible impatience of very senior executives, frame the results of their analysis in such a way as to avoid being 'shot as the bearers of bad news'.

In Chapter 5 we considered the work of Hofstede, Trompenaars and Hampden-Turner in which they highlight the need for geographic cultural sensitivity and understanding in team-based organisations. These considerations are equally true in acquisitions and mergers across geographic divides. Their research should help organisations to conduct due diligence with regard to possible difficulties due to geographic cultural differences.

Human resources due diligence can help acquirers to identify serious cultural differences, uncover competency gaps, and help define decision-making processes including who must be kept, who should go, and who runs reconfigured businesses. Cisco, acknowledged as one of the most successful M&A practitioners today, has senior HR professionals dedicated to due diligence and integration support.

Companies need to devote time and effort to due diligence in order to avoid surprises during the integration process or potentially nastier surprises later upon discovering environmental 'skeletons in cupboards' or frustrations as it emerges that the two organisations have fundamentally different cultures. Merger failures often result from a lack of careful evaluation of both the hard financial and soft personnel and organisational issues that are critical to organisational success (Epstein 2005).

Phase 3: Pre-Integration Planning

Research suggests that an array of key issues such as corporate brand strategies, organisation structures and decision-making processes only receive serious attention after the deal is announced (Ettenson and Knowles 2006).

Careful preparation is essential before the announcement, as a planning vacuum is likely to lead to political gamesmanship and not unreasonable efforts of self preservation. It is vital to clarify roles and responsibilities, decision-making processes and critical success factors as quickly as possible. Once such key decisions are made and goals and timetables set, managers can meet to plan many other integration issues in an environment of greater clarity and certainty.

As was discussed at the outset of this chapter, not all M&As are the same. Thus it follows that integration planning will be different in every case. In some cases, where the form of organisational structure is predetermined (e.g. the umpteenth Cisco Systems acquisition), planning will likely focus on post-integration organisation change management. In other cases, however, the form of organisational structure and branding is less obvious at the outset and different options should be carefully explored and determined during this pre-integration phase. In the situation of a 'merger of equals', a full range of options on structure and corporate branding should be considered rather than being constrained by either of the previous forms.

Corporate and product branding are key aspects of pre-integration planning. Clarity in brand strategy early on in the process can greatly help the integration of the organisations by sending the right signals to people both inside and outside each of the organisations. The right brand strategy can help clarify the goal of the merger or acquisition and support productive relationships between employees, customers and investors of both organisations (Ettenson and Knowles 2006).

The potential savings for integrating supply chains in M&As can be quite substantial and so also need to be fully explored and determined during the pre-integration planning phase. Working with such amalgamations as Cingular Wireless and AT&T Wireless, Unilever and Best Foods, and many others, consulting firm Accenture has observed that the competency of the combining entities in integrating their supply chains was a major factor in creating M&A value. In one of the biggest and most high-profile amalgamations in recent years, Hewlett Packard and Compaq achieved more than $1 billion in cost savings resulting from integrating supply chains. This represented almost half of the total cost savings in the amalgamation (Herd, Saksena and Steger 2005).

Some countries and/or economic regions such as the European Union have laws specifically governing employees' rights in the event of the transfer of a business or part of a business from one employer to another. These regulations must be carefully considered and addressed as part of the pre-integration planning process.

Communication must also be carefully planned and coordinated for the wide variety of audiences: customers, shareholders, employees, trade unions, and the media. Too often communication is late and too scant. Organisations frequently communicate the nature of the merger or acquisition (the 'what') but sometimes do not fully communicate the rationale for the M&A (the 'why'). If the rationale for change is fully explained and employees understand and believe it, the organisation is a long way towards implementing the change.

Phase 4: Post-Announcement Integration Planning and Change Management

The post-announcement integration planning phase calls for a continuation of careful planning from the previous phase but the process now includes the execution of the strategic intent. Immediate post-announcement actions will include customer visits and briefings, as well as well-choreographed employee briefings ensuring that employees hear the same message at the same time and from the right source.

The better the pre-integration planning in Phase 3, the clearer and more complete the message to all stakeholders. Immediately post-announcement can be a period of exhilaration for some, but it is a period of high stress and anxiety for many constituencies, including employees, customers and suppliers. The extent to which communicators can provide clear information and explain decisions made will go some way to alleviating some of that stress. Understandably, organisations will not have all the answers at the outset but should be able to explain ongoing processes and timeframes when additional decisions and further information will be available.

Customer management is critical during this period because it is not 'business as usual'. Customer service and communication is more critical than ever as it is not unusual for competitor organisations to capitalise on any uncertainty (Epstein 2005).

The early months following announcement (sometimes referred to as the first 100 days) is a critical time and all parts of the newly amalgamated organisation need to have the necessary information, resources and commitment to address the many issues that will inevitably arise, and do so at speed. Plans must be balanced and integrated between growing revenue on the one hand, while reducing cost on the other hand, while at the same time maintaining as much organisational calmness and focus on business fundamentals as is possible, given the circumstances.

Theory & Practice

In Canada, in 2002, a joint senior management 'integration team' of Deloitte & Touche and Arthur Anderson personnel carefully and effectively planned for the integration of over 1,000 Anderson employees into Deloitte.

On 31 May 2002 at 5.00 p.m. Pacific Time, Anderson Canada went 'dark'. All Anderson systems including phones, personal computers and e-mail were disconnected from the Anderson worldwide system. This marked the beginning of the integration into the Deloitte organisation. So detailed and effective was their implementation planning that, despite the fact that there were significant differences in their respective IT systems, the majority of these integrating employees had their computers reconfigured to the Deloitte systems with new e-mail addresses, a new phone number and business cards to give to their clients by the end of the following Monday, 3 June. (Mark 2003)

Integration teams will usually stay very close to the integration process until all parameters are met, up to and including shipment of the acquired company's products and invoicing under the amalgamated company's brand.

To build commitment to the change, there needs to be ongoing and endless communication. Kotter (1990) suggests that the three most important activities in managing change are communication, communication and communication. Companies who manage M&A integrations continuously use an array of communication vehicles to keep people up-to-date, especially during this period of major change and anxiety. These can include chief executive video briefings, management briefings, published bulletins and websites. Because effective employee communication is not always restricted to 'top down', some organisations have also commissioned employee surveys in order to understand how employees at different levels are responding to the changes.

We return to the subject of managing change in Chapter 8.

Structuring for M&A Integration

Deciding how best to structure an acquisition is one of the most important decisions to be made in the entire acquisition process. Integrating an acquisition into the existing acquiring company structure may work in the case of Cisco Systems, where the objective is typically to acquire a small company with an emerging technology. However, when Boeing acquired the aerospace manufacturer and defence contractor McDonnell Douglas in 1997, its objective was to leverage McDonnell Douglas's core competency in working with military customers. To maintain and build on that leverage, Boeing allowed McDonnell Douglas to become a stand-alone military business unit, with its own stand-alone operations.

The key to the decision, about how best to structure an acquisition, must go back to the original strategic intent. In the case of Cisco, the objective was to supplement R&D activities. In the case of Boeing, the objective was to acquire a business that had a critical core competency to be fostered and leveraged.

When Ben & Jerry's was acquired by Unilever in 2000, it immediately became a division of Unilever. Ben & Jerry's Chief Executive Perry Odak stepped down and founders Ben Cohen and Jerry Greenfield relinquished any remaining responsibility, other than to become 'ambassadors for the brand', which had been prescribed under the purchase agreement. In Ben & Jerry's, Unilever saw a company with a strong growth potential not only in the US but internationally, where its brand had become well-known in the premium ice-cream segment. In taking over the business, Unilever also saw significant cost reduction opportunities in applying more efficient supply chain methodologies (Austin and Quin 2007). Finally, Ben & Jerry's, with their reputation for commitment to social and 'green' causes, presents Unilever with a form of ethical brand imagery, which has been identified as a potential 'engine' for future growth.

Theory & Practice

Cisco Systems has established itself as a stellar performer in successful acquisitions. With revenues of $28 billion in 2006, Cisco holds the dominant market position in networking and communications technology and services. While the company invests substantial amounts in internal R&D (over 17 per cent of revenues in 2001), Cisco has achieved its dominant position through continuous acquisition.

As Cisco seek acquisitions to supplement their R&D activities to fuel their explosive growth, they focus primarily on the acquisition of small emerging businesses with exciting new technologies. They find that they are able to attract these businesses and, as importantly, retain the engineering entrepreneurs who founded these fledgling companies. Well aware of the long list of disappointing M&As in and around Silicon Valley, Cisco also take the view that the integration of their acquisitions are likely to be more successful if they focus on small emerging companies rather than larger ones.

As Cisco built a core competency in acquisitions integration, they began to formalise the process and make it more explicit (Nonaka 2001). As informal discussions and courtship move to expressions of serious intent by both parties, HR due diligence commences. Cisco's HR group checks the backgrounds of the key individuals in the prospective acquiree and takes a view

---

of the capacity of the individuals to contribute to and work in the larger Cisco organisation, and also seeks to understand their immediate career intentions post-acquisition. Often, their prospective employment terms and conditions form part of the overall purchase agreement. Stock options in Cisco and the vesting schedule are also important aspects to be determined. The HR team will begin planning for employee information, payroll and benefits integration. In parallel with this HR exploration, the acquiree's technology, finances, sales and, where relevant, supply chains are also closely examined.

With an agreement imminent, typically two months before the acquisition announcement, integration planning commences. A Cisco dedicated business integration unit forms a team of PR, sales and marketing, and HR personnel from both companies. This team is charged with the detailed planning and execution of the integration to a well-defined and proven recipe. The business integration team stays with the project until all parameters are met, up to and including shipment and invoicing of the acquired company's products under Cisco livery. (Mayer 2004)

The list of M&A headline grabbers is endless: GlaxoSmithKline; the post deregulation marriage of NYNEX-Bell Atlantic; HP and Compaq; JP Morgan and Chase Manhattan; Bank of America's acquisition of MBNA; GE's purchase of NBC; Murdoch's acquisitions trail in Europe, Australia and the US; Cisco's continuous acquisitions; Boeing's purchase of McDonnell Douglas; and P&G's acquisition of Gillette. The only certainty is that the list will continue to grow.

Clearly, each different merger or acquisition represents a very different strategic intent, each with its own unique set of opportunities and challenges. The manner in which M&A opportunities are properly targeted, explored through due diligence, planned for, integrated and structured must be determined by that strategic intent. Structuring the integration in a way that allows the acquired asset or competency to flourish is essential. Boeing's decision to allow McDonnell Douglas to be a stand-alone military business is a good example of a structure decision that allows them to achieve full leverage of that company's core competency of working directly with military customers.

Case Based on Chapter 7

Craigstone Construction Materials, based near Edinburgh, Scotland, is in the top ten UK suppliers of primary construction materials, including ready-mix concrete, pre-cast concrete, bricks and blocks, and tiles.

Background

The construction materials industry is quite cyclical with cycles typically running seven to eight years peak to peak. The industry is also fragmented because:

- Building materials have very high weight and bulk to value ratio with disproportionately high transportation costs. This means that the normal rules of economies of scale do not work as suppliers need to produce their product reasonably adjacent to the customer requirement (typically less than 100 miles).
- Products tend to be different due to regional architectural differences and local government building regulations.
- Influenced by the two points above, business relationships between architects, builders, developers and materials suppliers tend to be localised.

As a result, construction material providers generally tended to be small, private, family-run businesses.

While the industry has been characterised by traditional, fragmented, localised markets, a number of large international companies have emerged over time including Blue Circle, CRH, LaFarge, and Holderbank.

The Situation

From its modest beginnings outside Edinburgh after WWII, Craigstone has established itself as a very successful, middle-tier, materials provider across the UK. Encouraged by the success of the international players, Craigstone have just announced their first two international acquisitions:

1. Wroclaw Construction (Wroclaw, Poland): for €20 million; owner-managed; thirty-five employees; products include ready-mix concrete and pre-cast concrete.
2. Potsdamer Building Materials (Berlin, Germany): for €25 million; owner managed; fifty employees; products include pre-cast concrete, concrete masonry, bricks and tiles.

In both acquisition deals, Craigstone still has to decide whether or not to retain the owner-manager as part of the purchase agreement. Craigstone views these new European acquisitions as important stepping stones to becoming a successful pan-European construction materials provider.

Questions
1. What are the organisational structure design options open to Craigstone as it seeks to integrate these new acquisitions and potentially others in the medium term?
2. What design would you recommend and why? Include considerations around the centralisation-decentralisation continuum in your answer.
3. What would you recommend to Craigstone regarding the retention or otherwise of the owner-managers?

CHAPTER 8

MANAGING ORGANISATIONAL CHANGE

Introduction

Respected business author and organisational anthropologist Charles Handy offers a provocative, if somewhat graphic, metaphor for organisational change: if you put a frog into a pot of cold water and slowly heat it, the frog will let itself be boiled to death (1995). Handy's metaphor warns that our environment, just like the temperature of the pot with the frog, is constantly changing, sometimes imperceptibly so, and that organisations must be aware of even subtle changes in their environment and be able to respond to those changes accordingly or, like the frog, they too will not survive.

However, resistance and barriers to organisational change abound, including but certainly not limited to, threats to power and influence, fear of the unknown, inertia, organisational culture, organisation design, and so on. The list is endless. For many employees, including many managers, change is neither sought nor welcome. It is often disruptive and intrusive, and upsets balance. It can be confusing and loaded with paradox and contradictions. Successful change requires so much more than clever mottos, buzzwords and new t-shirts!

Tichey warns that all definitions of change are problematic. He explains that they are based on the assumption that we can differentiate between states of change and stability: 'This turns out to be not so simple. For organisations are always changing, often in subtle and incremental ways' (1983: 17). Jick (1993) and Porter (1980) capture this active and dynamic nature of organisational change when they speak of *positioning* and *adjusting* the organisation to achieve strategic fit with external forces of threats and opportunities.

This chapter reviews change management as a broad and generic construct. Chapter 9 goes on to apply change management principles specifically to organisation design and restructuring. Accordingly, this chapter considers different types and forms of organisational change; examines change models and posits essentials for successful change; explores the notion that change represents a transitional *process,* not just an *event*; and considers models for effectively managing organisational change.

Forms of Organisational Change

Not all organisational change is the same. There are different scales of change effort and, just like the athlete in training, it is important to understand whether you are competing in a marathon or a sprint. General Electric's (GE) introduction of Six Sigma has been described as an *incremental* process improvement methodology across the company and is very different from Citibank's first introduction of automatic teller machines, which *transformed* how customers conducted their routine banking. Jick (1995) describes transformational or radical change as a 'long march', where there is a radical transformation of the organisation's mission. A long march would aptly describe Nokia's re-invention of itself from a producer of paper products and rubber boots to the high-tech telecommunications supplier it is today.

Models of Change Management

Over the years, change management focused on identifying sources of resistance to change and offered ways to overcome that resistance. However, in the last decade or so, contributions have been increasingly aimed at creating visions and desired futures, gaining political support for them and managing the progress of the organisation towards them. Two such highly regarded models of change are summarised here.

1. Kotter (1995) offers eight steps to organisational change:

    a) *Establish a sense of urgency.*
       Highlight potential opportunities or threats. Communicate this information clearly and dramatically. Explain the consequences of not changing.

b) *Form a powerful coalition.*
   Convince and 'sign-up' organisational and opinion leaders of critically important constituencies. Encourage the key participants to work as a team.

c) *Create a vision.*
   Develop a compelling picture of a future that appeals to the important stakeholder constituencies.

d) *Communicate the vision.*
   Use every possible communication vehicle to communicate the new vision and strategies. The message needs to be woven into day-to-day discussions and explanations, over and over again.

e) *Empower others to act on the vision.*
   Encourage managers and employees to take bold steps to actualise the vision. Remove barriers and obstacles that hinder employees taking initiative in pursuit of the vision. Encourage risk taking.

f) *Plan for and create short-term wins.*
   Significant change takes some time and employees need to be reassured that the organisation is on the right path. Early wins reinforce commitment to the 'long march'. Recognise and reward the success of the early participants.

g) *Consolidate improvements.*
   While early successes and wins should be recognised and celebrated, 'declaring the war to be over' too soon is catastrophic. New approaches are very fragile and subject to regression.

h) *Institutionalise new approaches.*
   Help employees make the connection between the new behaviours and the outcomes. Create and nurture openness to ongoing change. Until new behaviours are well-rooted in behavioural norms and shared values, they are subject to degradation as soon as the pressure for change wears off. Make sure that the next generation of managers really does personify the changes and new approaches.

2. Ulrich and colleagues (1997), working with GE executives, developed a change model for that organisation that has many

similarities with the Kotter model. The main differences between the two models are really points of emphasis, e.g. Kotter places emphasis on communication, Ulrich *et al.* on modifications of systems and structures.

a) *Change leader (who?).*
   A leader who owns and champions the change; makes public commitments to making it happen; will garner resources to sustain it; and will put in the personal time and attention to follow it through.

b) *Create a shared need (why?).*
   Build a compelling need for change; show why the change is necessary and how the change will help.

c) *Shape the vision (what?).*
   Describe what the outcome will be when the change is implemented. Develop a picture of the future state that is relatively easy to communicate and appeals to the key stakeholders.

d) *Mobilise commitment (who else?).*
   Similar to Kotter's 'powerful guiding coalition', this model also stresses the need to identify the key opinion leaders and those with the necessary power and influence to actively support the change.

e) *Modify systems and structures (how will the change be rooted?).*
   Understand how the change can be helped or hindered by existing processes and systems, and modify as necessary. This may include an examination of the organisational cultural norms and HR processes such as recognition and rewards.

f) *Monitor progress (how will the change outcomes be monitored?).*
   Develop a few key measurements to indicate the ongoing success or otherwise of the change initiative; this may include comparative benchmarking.

g) *Make it last (how to keep focus on the change?).*
   Again, similar to Kotter's model, determine how best to institutionalise the change, and an openness and commitment to ongoing change.

Essentials for Organisational Change

The similarities between the Kotter and the Ulrich *et al.* GE model are echoed in much of the organisational change literature. In summarising some leading authors of organisational change, the following emerge as important prerequisites for successful organisational change.

1. Strong, Visible Leadership

Changing an organisational structure requires strong, visible leadership to guide the change, to enroll members in the new structure and direction and confront those managers not visibly supporting or simply playing lip-service to the change.

Large-scale organisational change requires a strong, visible leader to communicate the need for change in a clear and compelling way and to visibly lead by example and with constancy of purpose.

It would be unusual, if not impossible, for the chief executive alone to provide all the leadership for the change effort. Any lack of substantive and visible support for the change by other senior members of the management team will quickly become apparent to the organisation. The degree to which individual members of senior management truly buy into the change and can describe it in consistent terms is a litmus test for the probability of success. A lack of visible collective commitment is likely to raise doubts and erode confidence in the planned change.

Theory & Practice

The manufacturing organisation of a large European high-tech company had just finalised a planned reorganisation. Functions and responsibilities previously embedded in each of the plants at the different locations were now going to be centralised in order to achieve scale in negotiation with third-party outsource partners.

The site general managers participated in the reorganisation evaluation and decision-making process. Not surprisingly, views on the proposed change ranged from wholehearted agreement to disagreement. Through substantial and ardent debate over several meetings, there was movement towards a consensus, ranging from positive support to quiet acquiescence around the table.

A conference of all manufacturing managers was convened to announce the new organisation and structure and, while the chief executive explained the need for the change and some high-level architecture, much of the detailed presentations were delivered by the site general managers 'all singing from the same hymn sheet', each reinforcing the others' presentations. Follow-up meetings were held at each site, again explaining the changes and the rationale for them. General managers from the other sites attended each of these site meetings.

Without such highly visible collective support for the changes, it was feared that a minority of general managers would appear to support the changes with almost silent acquiescence during the early debates but might engage in subtle defence mechanisms including passive-aggressive behaviour once back at their own site. The manner in which the announcement was communicated with the site general managers as the core communicators largely negated the opportunity for some general managers to engage in such defence mechanisms later on. However, one general manager, who struggled with the new structure and the seeming diminution of his role, did resign and found another opportunity externally.

A further example relates to when Greg Dyke and his senior colleagues introduced a major organisational change at the BBC. In this instance, he and his senior colleagues made sure the change was led by themselves and not by external consultants. Over the years, the BBC had used consultants frequently to support management change initiatives. One senior manager suggested that the BBC had an antibody resistance to consultants. The problem is that when consultants are used, there is sometimes a temptation to defer to their expert knowledge. Change programmes sometimes fail because organisations follow consultancy 'packaged' processes that are not rooted in or connected to their own realities and context. This is not to say that consultants do not have important support roles in advising and guiding executive management on the implementation of change, but they cannot be looked at to provide the essential, visible leadership for the change.

2. Strong Support for Change

In addition to the key decision makers, it is essential to identify and enroll other key stakeholders in the change process. In most cases, leadership cannot bring about effective change on its own and, to be successful, change efforts must have the solid support of other key constituencies. There is a need to form a powerful guiding coalition, where individuals with enough power and influence are identified and aligned to support the change (Kotter 1995). Occasionally, some of these stakeholders are not members of the management group (e.g. a board member or a key customer). As a result, the influencing process may need to operate more informally and outside the normal hierarchical protocols and boundaries.

It is important to understand the sources and potency of support for change. One method to analyse the source and potency of support is to populate the key stakeholders across a grid, which measures power and influence on one axis and level of support on the other axis. Such an analysis identifies where to disproportionately invest time and effort to support the change. Figure 8.1 is an example of this analysis.

Figure 8.1: Stakeholder Analysis I

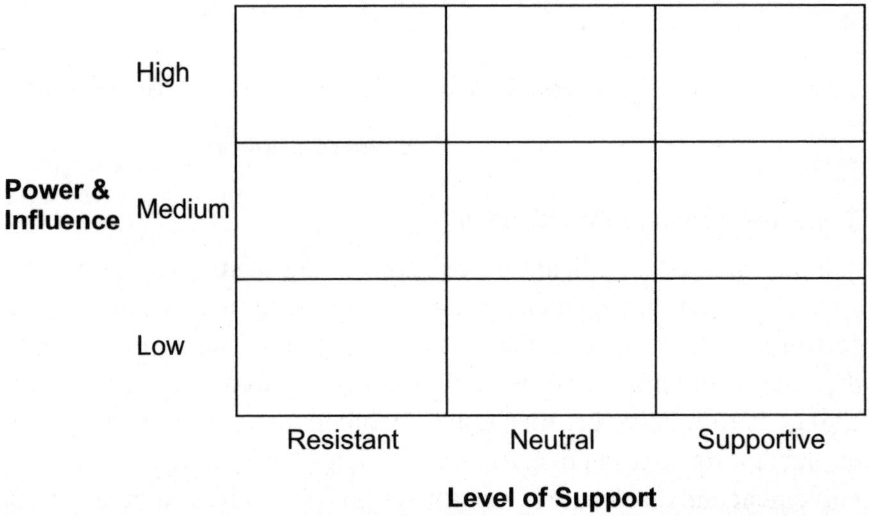

Power & Influence		Resistant	Neutral	Supportive
	High			
	Medium			
	Low			

Level of Support

Figure 8.2 shows a simple example of a distribution of stakeholders in this context. While the effort to drive change should be aimed across the entire community, a *disproportionate* effort should be focused on converting Joan, who has high power and influence, to move from being neutral to being supportive. Equally, Mary, who has medium power and influence, should be targeted to convert from her neutral position to being supportive. It may also be possible to move Mike and, somewhat less importantly, Margaret, from positions of being resistant to at least being neutral.

**Figure 8.2: Stakeholder Analysis II –
Disproportionate Attention**

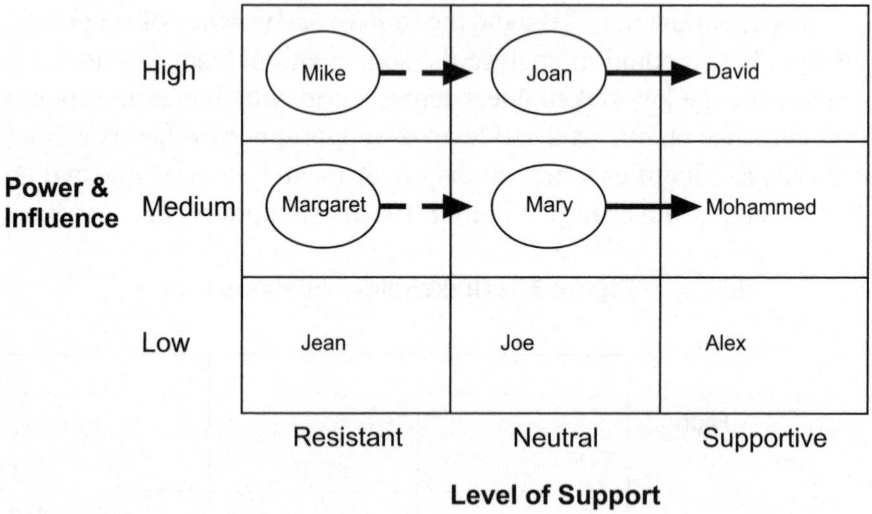

Power & Influence		Resistant	Neutral	Supportive
	High	Mike →	Joan →	David
	Medium	Margaret →	Mary →	Mohammed
	Low	Jean	Joe	Alex

Level of Support

3. Involvement and Participation?

Another area of significant agreement among leading authors in the area of change management is the need for early involvement on the part of the constituencies that are most affected. These authors agree that one of the most effective strategies for overcoming resistance to change is to involve organisational members directly in planning and implementing that change. However, Jick (1993) notes that full involvement and disclosure is not always possible. There are likely to be circumstances where wide involvement is simply not an option. Some of the most successful change efforts were born out of crisis, requiring urgent action, thus offering little or no opportunity for organisation-wide engagement and involvement. Structural reorganisation tends to be an area of organisational change that is 'tops down', with a short window of time for execution.

Theory & Practice

The potential demise faced by British Airways in the 1980s is such an example of crisis-driven change. In September 1981, BA's Chief Executive Roy Watts issued a bulletin to all employees: 'BA is facing the worst crisis in its history. Unless we take swift and remedial action now, we are heading for a loss of at least £100 million pounds this year. No business can survive losses of this scale. Unless we take decisive action now, there is a real possibility that BA will go out of business for lack of money. We have to cut our costs sharply and have to cut them fast. We have no more choice and no more time.' (Jick 1993: 48)

Watts was successful in achieving the necessary cost savings at British Airways and at the same time began to build an excellent customer service product over the following decade, proclaiming BA to be the 'world's favourite airline'.

Organisation-wide change programmes that focus on structure design involve redefining people's positions and roles. The case study in Chapter 3 considered a reorganisation of structure from a functional organisation to a strategic business unit structure. The former structure had experienced and talented functional specialists in each of the key roles. However, the new structure would require individuals with quite different skills and competencies. Those skills and competencies that served ahead of manufacturing or sales so well in the past are not necessarily the same skills for success in managing a successful strategic business unit in the future.

Reorganisations, by their nature, tend to affect more senior level managers in the organisation. A production operative or supervisor may not be directly affected by a decision to centralise manufacturing globally. On the other hand, such a change most certainly affects the plant manager and other senior personnel. It is reasonable for individuals in this senior group to be unduly preoccupied with self interest or 'my' issues, for example, my job, my promotion prospects, my new boss, and my very occupational survival! Given that very human response, it is difficult to actively engage and involve managers who are directly impacted by the change.

Organisational change will have a much greater chance of success if the people responsible for implementing the change feel they were consulted and contributed their ideas to the change. For this to happen in the context of organisational restructuring, it is important to clarify roles and responsibilities, decision-making processes and critical success factors as quickly as possible. Without such clarity, there is the potential for self-interested organisational politics and gamesmanship. Once such key decisions are clarified and goals and timetables set, managers can meet to plan the many facets of the new structure.

4. Effective Communication

One of the strongest areas of agreement among leading writers on organisational change is the need for effective communication. However, managers must understand that communication is not about the transmission of the message but instead concerns the effective reception of the message. Some managers feel communication is complete when they pin the notice on the bulletin board. Effective managers engage in conversations with their employees and weave the message into day-to-day discussions, making sure employees really understand the message.

Effective managers root discussions about performance in the context of the 'bigger picture' and turn boring and unread company communications into open dialogue about the change. Those effective managers take 'ritualistic and tedious' quarterly management meetings and turn them into exciting and animated discussions on the change (Kotter 1995). Effective managers spend as much time on the 'why' or rationale for the change as they do on the 'what' or nature of the change. These managers find that, where employees really understand the compelling rationale for the change, they are already half-way towards achieving the change. Only by carefully listening to employee concerns and seeking to address those concerns will management be best positioned to promote active cooperation and participation.

5. Training and Education

Some forms of reorganisation (e.g. introduction of team-based structures) need to be supported by employee training and education. Organisational changes regularly require new knowledge and competencies at all levels in the organisation. In many cases, the desired changes cannot take effect if the employees do not have the necessary skills and knowledge. Educational activities can help employees understand the need for the change and can help build greater commitment to that change.

Often, training needs to address not only the technical aspects of the work but also needs to address the social skills to be developed. For example, as many change programmes seek to promote greater teamwork, it is essential that the team members receive the necessary social skills training to operate effectively in such a setting.

Finally, timing appears to be important. Education and training is likely to be more effective if the student has an immediate opportunity to practice the lesson. There are plenty of examples of companies who provided extensive education at the launch of a change programme, while six months to a year would pass before the employees had the opportunity to engage in the actual changed activity. In such cases, much of the learning had evaporated in the meantime.

6. Detailed Implementation Plan

Vision and desired future states are, by their very nature, broad and 'big picture'. They can be quite general when compared to the detailed specifics necessary to actualise the vision. It is essential to translate 'big picture' scenarios into very detailed implementation plans. Such plans should identify the critical activities and events during the transition. The plans should specify the who, what, where, when and how.

Change sometimes requires movement to a transitional state. Because it can be difficult for a stable organisation to change itself, it is sometimes necessary to create temporary systems to accomplish the transition. One of the most common mechanisms is the creation of a 'steering committee' as a parallel structure to help guide and direct the change.

7. Assessment of Organisational Processes

Changes intended to improve performance in one part of the organisation may affect other parts of the organisation with surprising, and often unintended, negative consequences. It is important to comprehend that a change to part of an organisation impacts on other parts of the organisation and on the organisation as a whole. Also, existing processes should be re-appraised to ensure that they are aligned to and in support of the proposed change. For example, many organisations are striving for the development of teams and team structures. However, many of these organisations' performance appraisal systems may still be based on the more traditional principle of assessing the employee as an individual.

This detailed assessment needs to be completed to ensure that the proposed change (a) does not create unforeseen and unintended consequences in other key areas of the organisation, and (b) current processes are reviewed and adjusted where necessary, to ensure that they are in harmony with the proposed change. Otherwise, change efforts run the very real risk of creating poor fit among organisational components, the result of which is either failure of the change effort or a decrease in organisational efficiency.

It is also recommended that an assessment be made of the amount of change being undertaken at a period in time. There have to be limits to an organisation's capacity to handle change at any one time. It is possible to consider delaying a change initiative until a previously deployed key change has been fully implemented. Managers and supervisors need to understand the implications of multi-year strategies so that they can best plan how much to absorb and change.

8. Publicise Results and Provide Rewards and Recognition

As already noted, people will not sustain long marches unless they see compelling evidence within twelve to twenty-four months that the journey is producing expected results. An early sense of urgency is likely to dissipate over a long period unless there are clear indications that the organisation is on the right path. In supporting a change, employees often make some sacrifices and it is highly reinforcing to see that sacrifices produce dividends. It is important therefore that early wins are actively planned for (versus passively hoped for) in the change process. Results should be widely published and participants well recognised and rewarded.

There is an obvious psychological boost in achieving early wins. It not only creates energy for further wins but also has the effect of enrolling a higher level of involvement of those more passively connected to the process. People generally like to win and, as in sport, winning gathers a wider range of active supporters. Consequently, it is essential that the early wins are highly publicised and that the participants receive a high level of recognition.

However, there is a danger that, in recognising early wins, victory is declared too soon. As already noted, declaring the war won too early can be catastrophic. Great care needs to be exercised to ensure that employees see these wins as positive landmarks on the correct route, but that there is still much of the journey to be completed. Until the change can diffuse itself into the culture of the organisation over a sustained period, it is subject to regression.

A powerful way of reinforcing a change in priorities is to change the reward system. Too often, organisations actually encourage resistance by maintaining a reward system that is inconsistent with the desired change (Beckhard and Harris 1987). An Ernst & Young study found that in the motor, computer, banking and healthcare industries, which were all driving for greater quality, actual quality performance impacted pay in fewer than 20 per cent of organisations. It is surprising that so many organisations expect individuals to behave in certain ways, especially in transition, while rewarding them for actual behaviours that are in conflict with the espoused behaviours.

Promotion decisions tell an organisation a great deal about the behaviours that are really valued. To promote those who demonstrate negative or even passive behaviour towards the change effort sends a serious mixed message to the entire organisation. Leaders must understand the new behaviours and competencies required to support the change, and promote people accordingly. There can be few more influential ways to reinforce positive behaviours than the organisation observing some early wins being recognised by management and the early promotion of the active participants. Such promotions and, perhaps as importantly, removing or reassigning existing managers who do not exhibit these espoused behaviours, shows how serious an organisation is about the change.

9. Develop Effective Feedback and Diagnostic Tools

Organisations need responsive and sensitive feedback control loops to gather information on the 'vital signs' of progress throughout the change and as a mechanism to diagnose variation from the plan. It is not sufficient for leaders to identify the need for change and to generate involvement, and so on. They also need to ensure that the change is proceeding on course. Some chief executives make the mistake of assuming that by simply articulating the need for change, change will follow. This wishful thinking ignores many of the interests and agendas that abound in organisational life. There is much evidence about senior managers ordering change and assuming such changes follow. These situations happen because leaders lack effective feedback devices to tell them whether actions have been effective or not.

10. Reinforce and Institutionalise the Change

Until new behaviours are rooted in social norms and shared values, they are subject to degradation as soon as the pressure for change is removed (Kotter 1995). Structures and practices need to be established in order to continuously reinforce and institutionalise the change. Change can be tested when senior managers are replaced. To sustain the change, it is essential that the change has been institutionalised into the very culture of the organisation. Hewlett Packard Inc. has often been cited as an organisation that works hard to institutionalise change into its culture and describes this culture as 'the HP Way'. Practices of recognition and reward go a long way to support the process of reinforcement and institutionalisation.

Jick (1993) offers an important additional concept in institutionalising change. He offers advice that it is not the actual change that needs to be institutionalised, for this change may itself have to be changed in the future. He notes that, instead of making one specific change, organisations need to create an environment that identifies and accepts the continuing necessity of change.

There appears to be a high level of agreement in the organisational change literature regarding the important components of a successful change methodology. All of these components have a significant role in managing change; each is a key piece in the jigsaw. Leadership, supportive coalitions, and action plans only produce confusion without a vision. Leadership, vision, coalitions, and action plans that do not include the provision of skills and competencies only produce anxiety. The lack of an implementation plan produces false starts and the lack of resources and sponsorship produces frustration.

Organisational Change is a Process, not an Event

Bridges (1991) reminds us that change is really about transitions and the psychological process people go through to come to terms with a changed situation. At a personal level, the death of a near relative or a divorce may be an event that causes upheaval, however it is the difficult and often lengthy transition that results from such an event that people find so hard to manage. Bridges advises that the starting point for transition is not a new beginning but the acceptance of endings to leave the old situation behind.

Theory & Practice

Recognising this need to start with an ending, it is reported that Hewlett Packard, when acquiring Apollo Computer in Massachusetts in 1989, organised what could only be described as a 'wake' at the acquired site. At the event, the transitioning employees were encouraged to take something from the old organisation (pen, business card, and so on) and throw it into a large bonfire, thereby beginning to mark the ending. There is nothing to suggest that this 'wake' was their only transitional effort but it serves to highlight that they recognised that psychological transition depends on letting go of the old situation.

Typically, it is not the changes themselves that people resist, but the loss and endings that occur as a result of such changes. Bridges reminds us of the Spanish conquistador Hernán Cortés who dealt effectively and dramatically with such a situation. When Cortés landed in Veracruz with his men he realised that they were fearful, if not hopeless, about their situation. In order to have his men focus on their immediate challenges and futures, Cortés burned his ships.

There is a widely accepted model of how people respond to change, called the 'change U curve'.[1] The model suggests that people transition through the curve from left to right at different speeds. The goal for leaders is to help and encourage employees to move through the early stages as quickly as possible so that they can move on to the more positive, reconstructive stages of the change (see Figure 8.3).

Figure 8.3: An Example of a Typical Transitional Process

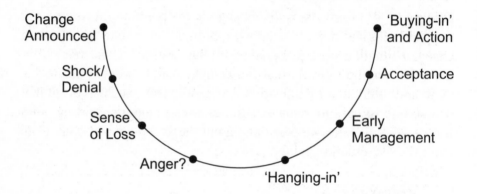

As was noted in the conclusion to Chapter 1, the focus of this book is on organisational structure. However, other important levers must also be aligned to support the change process. Such levers are detailed in the McKinsey '7S Model' and Galbraith's 'Star Model' and include such important elements as: people (core competencies, talent development, performance management); reward systems (promotions, pay and bonuses, recognition); and management values and behaviours and processes (order fulfilment, new product development, information processes, decision making).

According to Prahalad, 'Most managers have little appetite for either fundamentally rethinking strategy or creating radically new organisational capabilities' (2002: ix). On more than one occasion, when invited to review a client's organisational structure and human resources strategies, I suggested to the client managers that we should start the process by carefully considering the business strategy, only

---

[1] Origins uncertain

to find that there was no business strategy, other than a 'steady as she goes' aspiration.

Managing change is hard work, requiring strong and persistent leadership. It is a process that requires careful planning and thorough and deliberate execution through a proven methodology or 'change model'. Skipping steps only creates an illusion of greater speed and progress, often slowing momentum and cancelling hard-won gains. It must be managed as a transitional process rather than simply seen as an announcement to be pinned to the bulletin board or released on the intranet.

Every organisation undergoes change from time to time. It is usually difficult and expensive, involving radical changes in strategies and/or reorganisations, and changes in work design or deeply embedded organisational cultures and attitudes. However, despite the challenges of resistance, many organisations succeed in their change efforts. Organisations that continuously sense changes to their external and internal environments and have the capacity, agility and determination to respond to those changes have a decided competitive advantage over those that do not.

Change is about vision, convincing communication, persistence and hard work. It is 20 per cent inspiration and 80 per cent perspiration.

Case Based on Chapter 8

Acme Widgets & Tools Ltd. is an organisation largely comprised of acquisitions that have broad common technologies but are focused on substantially different markets and customers.

Background

In 2005, a new chief executive quickly identified a highly divisionalised, competitive culture and silo mentality, which combined to impact negatively on product development and technology exchange. Among other things, he discovered that:

- There was substantial replication in motor design in many of the divisions.

- Each division subcontracted significant manufacturing to their own favourite subcontractor.
- None of the divisions had relationships with universities or advanced machine shop design consultancies to identify best design concepts, including ergonomics, and to enhance product operation, including attention to safety and reduction of operator fatigue and discomfort.

The new CEO valued the divisional structure, believing that the divisions best understood their markets and were best organised to service those markets and their customers. However, he was strongly of the opinion that he needed to break down the silo mentality and begin to actively share information and technical know-how. The company could not afford the extensive replication of effort that currently existed, which was adding to cost and delays in the introduction of new products. He needed to create a much greater level of collaboration, support and sharing of knowledge across the divisions.

The Response

While maintaining much of the autonomy and individuality of the divisions, the CEO established:

1. A Product Technology Forum. This group of engineering leaders from across the divisions was charged with:

   a) Reducing the number of motors across all divisions from eighteen to five fundamental standardised designs. Each division then had two years to migrate to these designs and could only design new products based on any of these five standards. No division could introduce a new motor for a new application without the express approval of the Forum and the CEO.

   b) Working in close collaboration with key universities and advanced machine shop design consultancies to identify best design concepts, including ergonomics, to enhance product operation, including safety, and reduce operator fatigue and discomfort.

   c) In conjunction with b) above, establish and maintain a centralised data warehouse for product design and all related matters. This electronic library would combine the information of all the divisions, providing easy access to employees in all the divisions.

2. A Procurement Forum. This small group of senior procurement executives, product engineers, and quality engineers were charged with:

   a) Standardising subcontracting procedures across the company.
   b) Negotiating with all current subcontractors (fourteen) with a goal to reducing the number to two for each of three broad technology areas (for a total of six). Such selections were to be based on price, quality and on-time delivery.
   c) In conjunction with 1(c) above, working with the smaller number of preferred suppliers to populate the 'data warehouse' so that division product designers could access subcontractor technological capabilities and standards.

The degree of difficulty in managing these organisational changes cannot be overstated. Divisional general managers and their respective staffs resented the restrictions. They felt that they knew best what the customer wanted and were unhappy with being restricted to the five standard motors. Equally, they believed that their subcontractor was the best and they had built up excellent relationships at a personal level with the management of that company, sometimes enhanced through generous corporate entertainment.

The CEO and his advisors were concerned that, unless there was significant authority given to the two forums, they would only be 'talking shop' with endless debate and no decisions, with much 'looking over their shoulder' at the divisional general managers. The CEO attended all the early meetings of both forums to ensure progress was being made. He reset the goals of the forum members to where the work of the group was their number one priority, with appropriate contingent rewards. He reset the goals of the divisional general managers around profitability growth and showed them that the two forums would be of enormous help to them in reducing costs and speeding up new product 'time to market'. He also reconfigured the bonus structure. Previously, the bonus for general managers was predicated solely on the profitability of their individual business unit. Going forward, their bonuses would be structured 50 per cent on the profitability of the overall company and 50 per cent based on the profitability of their individual business units.

Given time and occasional 'forceful leadership' by the CEO, the forums began to make a very effective contribution and a real difference in cost reduction and reduction of 'time to market' for new product introductions.

Questions

1. What were the really important actions or interventions that helped bring about a successful change?
2. What change principles applied and why?

CHAPTER 9

PLANNING FOR ORGANISATION DESIGN

This final chapter outlines the important steps in planning and executing an organisational restructuring, and draws together and summarises the key themes developed throughout the book.

> ### Hardly Theory & Practice!
> *For many of us, the Internet can be a constant source of humourous tales, swapped between family and friends. As a HR practitioner, consultant and former rower, the following tale has particular personal appeal. It tells the story of a Blue automobile company and a Red automobile company who decided to have a boat race between them on the Thames River, just outside London. Crews from both companies practiced hard both on and off the water to reach peak physical fitness. The race was held on a perfectly crisp and calm day and the Blue crew won by a proverbial mile.*
>
> *Corporate management of the Red crew were desperately disappointed with the result and were determined to find the reason for the defeat. A taskforce of very senior executives was formed to analyse the problem and recommend appropriate action. After much study and debate, the taskforce reported that the Blue crew had eight people rowing and one person steering, while the Red crew had eight people steering and one person rowing. Not wishing to rush to conclusions, the senior executives decided to bring in a consulting company to study the problem in more depth. After an extended period of analysis and substantial consultancy fees, the consultants*

> *concluded that too many of the crew were steering and not enough were rowing.*
>
> *The senior executives of the Red crew decided to redesign the structure of their crew. The new crew structure had one manager, two assistant managers, and five supervisors to guide, support and coach the sole remaining rower in the boat. Human resources also designed an incentive bonus plan to support the new structure. This plan paid managers a 20 per cent bonus, supervisors 10 per cent and the rower 5 per cent (his bonus would only be paid in the event of winning the race).*
>
> *A new race was organised and this time the Blue crew won by twice the winning margin of last time. Shortly afterwards, the Red company decided to 'downsize' and laid off the sole rower. The five supervisors and two assistant managers were reassigned and, given his seniority, the manager was promoted. The company sold the boat and oars to pay the consultant's bill.* (Adapted from Hellreigel *et al.* 1998: 574)

Organisation Design

The above far-fetched tall tale is presented as an allegory to depict the response of some organisations to symptoms of organisational difficulty in the form of a knee-jerk reaction to reorganise.

Organisation design is a basic tool available not just for executive management but for managers at all levels in the organisation. Managers must be aware of design concepts such as spans of control and hierarchical layers. Organisational re-designs make it possible to improve performance by shifting roles and responsibilities and by fostering interlinking relationships and networks. However, there is always the danger that some reorganisations amount to little more than a cosmetic exercise and little else happens beyond moving some of the organisation chart boxes around. In such cases, the organisational structure looks different but, sadly, performs much as it did before because none of the underlying problems are addressed. Successful companies reorganise and restructure based on how well the proposed organisation design directly meets the changing needs of their businesses. While the focal point of this book is to explore and examine organisational structure, other substantial levers of change or pieces of the organisational jigsaw must also be addressed in organisation design. Galbraith (2002) warns that there is a potential to spend too much time drawing charts and far too little time on the other jigsaw pieces of architecture. Ultimate success comes from a structure that is fully aligned to the business strategy but also aligned to the other key elements of organisational architecture including systems and processes, people management, technology and metrics.

Symptoms of ineffective organisation design include:

- Poorly defined roles and responsibilities, e.g. different marketing managers competing with each other for the same business opportunity.
- Lack of coordination, e.g. delays in 'time-to-market' for new products due to lack of coordination between hardware design, software development, and manufacturing.
- Excessive conflict, e.g. relationships across business units which have unnecessary levels of conflict, power struggles and gamesmanship.
- Duplication of scarce and expensive resources, e.g. different units not sharing expensive equipment or specialist staff.

In today's ever-changing business environment, the idea that an organisational structure could be effective beyond a decade is long gone. As noted in Chapter 6, one cannot but be impressed by Procter & Gamble's dynamic organisation designs. P&G continuously adjust their structures in order to cope with their fast-paced external (e.g. markets) and internal (e.g. acquisitions) environments. Changes in the business environment are compelling reasons for companies to seriously consider organisational redesign as a lever for organisational change. Regular exploration of organisational structure is important in order to:

- Pursue new business opportunities, including markets, geographic reach and acquisitions.

- Improve key business processes such as speed to market of new products, supply chain and customer service.
- Achieve greater organisational teamwork, knowledge-sharing and reduce excessive costs.

As explored in Chapter 7, the almost exponential growth in mergers and acquisitions has created a surge in organisation design in order to integrate businesses or indeed determine that the acquisition should operate as a stand-alone business.

Planning for Change: Organisation Design

Continuous change in the business environment and competitive landscape is the norm today. The ability of the firm to respond to changes in the way it reorganises to meet opportunities and threats is a source of significant competitive advantage. Key elements in planning organisational structural change include:

1. Alignment to Business Strategy

No one structure 'fits all'. Chapter 1 urges that structure must be influenced by the business strategy of an organisation. The leadership team needs to clarify the unique business proposition and the core competencies necessary to deliver that strategy. The organisational planning process should carefully consider the business strategy and explore structural elements that support the strategy. Issues of organisational complexity, business stability and so on, all have a direct bearing on structure choices.

Authors such as Miles and Snow (1986) and Porter (1980) highlight that low-cost strategies need a substantial efficiency-oriented structure including strong central authority and control, and highly efficient process management. Conversely, a differentiated strategy requires a flexible, loosely-knit structure with good horizontal coordination and with a strong emphasis on brand management and new product development.

2. Analysis of the Current Structure

There needs to be a detailed organisational analysis. This analysis should include an examination of current key processes, e.g. new product development, order fulfillment, and so on. This analysis should include a thorough exploration of weaknesses and performance gaps in those processes. It should also include how information flows, how decisions are made and by whom. The analysis should identify and highlight the weaknesses that the new structure must address.

3. Design the Structure

The leadership team should then develop and tailor a shortlist of possible structural designs necessary to support the business strategy, e.g. functional, business unit, geographic, matrix, and so on. In the process, they should define how work should be coordinated and integrated across the design elements. For each of the shortlisted designs, they should highlight the likely advantages and disadvantages of each design in the context of their business strategy.

An alternative approach would be to engage in an 'idealised design' process. In this approach, the leadership team envisions the perfect structure design as if it is starting from scratch. If they were designing the organisation with a blank sheet, drawing on their organisational knowledge, free from all politics, self interest and other impediments, how would they design the structure? Once the idealised design is completed, the leadership team works back to what is almost perfect but is still possible, allowing for some important trade-offs to reflect the realities of its business and organisation (Ackoff 2006).

4. Refine the Structure at the Detail Level and Project Planning

Oliver Wyman, international organisational consultants, advise that the best designs are those that emerge from the widest possible range of alternatives and the best design processes involve people who fully understand the organisation and its work. Once a 'high-level' structure has been defined and key interfaces clarified, it is important to establish a project team at the appropriate level to propose detailed refinements to the proposed structure and to consider and clarify unit and individual roles and responsibilities. In order to avoid the likelihood of preoccupation with 'my' issues (my role? my prospects?) referred to in Chapter 8, it is essential that such issues are defined and clarified for project team members in advance of their engagement in the project. Oliver Wyman add that the best designs are developed with implementation in mind.

5. Change Management Process

There needs to be a robust and effective change management methodology to ensure the successful execution of the new structure (see Chapter 8). Such a methodology needs to include leadership, the building of a supportive coalition, effective communication, effective feedback and diagnosis, and continuous reinforcement of the changes.

Conclusion

Structure needs to be aligned with strategy. Differing business environments and strategies impact on structural choices such as hierarchical layers and spans of control, and on functional or geographic designs and concepts of alignment and coordination. Rigid hierarchies, high levels of functional specialisation, narrow job descriptions, inflexible policies and procedures, and narrow traditional pay and reward practices are unlikely to facilitate the creation and reinforcement of a work environment that is flexible and adaptive.

The structure of an organisation is comprised of the roles, responsibilities, relationships and coordinating linkages that have been deliberately designed to support the business strategy. In so doing:

- It enables members of the organisation to understand and undertake a wide variety of responsibilities in a structure that delineates the specialisation and departmentalisation of roles, functions and tasks.
- It enables members of the organisation to coordinate their activities through integrating mechanisms such as hierarchical supervision, matrix-style integration, and policies and procedures.
- It defines the boundaries of the organisation and its interfaces with the environment, customers and suppliers and other organisations and institutions with which it must interact.

The fundamental elements of organisation design discussed and explored in the earlier chapters include:

1. *Structural mechanisms:* tall hierarchical structures with narrow spans of control are typically characterised by more centralised and slower decision making and more problematic communication flow. Flatter organisations, with wider spans of control, on the other hand, tend to be characterised by quicker, more decentralised decision making and better communication flow.

2. *Division of work:* organisations are typically structured by functional specialism, business unit or geography. Each of these has its own advantages and disadvantages. However, some of the disadvantages can be addressed by hybrid structures that have features of some of the other structural choices, e.g. business unit and geography. Whatever structural choice is made should be regularly reviewed for continuing relevance to the business strategy.

3. *Integrating mechanisms:* a direct consequence of the division of work is the need to coordinate and align the work of the different groups and individuals. Mechanisms to integrate and coordinate the work of different groups include matrix structures and networks. While matrix structures have the potential to facilitate coordination and support key interdependencies across different constituencies, such structures require a culture of collaborative teamwork and processes to reconcile priority conflicts.

   Informal networks are promoted to try to reduce inter-group rivalry and silo mentality. Organisations are social systems with relationships based on shared backgrounds and interests, friendships and maybe age groups. These informal relationships are just as important and real as the formal structures. Such associations and 'communities of practice' can encourage people with common interests to collaborate proactively and openly, and not be encumbered by hierarchy or departmental politics.

4. *Teamwork:* work teams represent a radical departure from traditional scientific management and conventional organisational structures. Studies show that team-based structures achieve higher levels of productivity, quality, customer service

and safety. However, the challenges of creating an effective team-based structure, including top management commitment and a significant investment in human resources processes, must not be underestimated.

Despite Chandler's (1962) urgings in the 1960s that structure follows strategy, it is only in the last decade or two that organisational structure design has gained recognition as an essential lever for strategy execution and organisational change. Most traditional organisations have been designed on the joint paradigms of Weber's machine bureaucracy and Taylor's scientific management. However, as organisations need to be decisive and respond quickly to their ever-changing environments, they are flattening their hierarchies, reorganising to get closer to markets and customers, applying team-based approaches to working together and drawing on the hidden power of social networks. At the other end of the evolutionary continuum to Weber and Taylor, organisations such as Dell and Amazon operate in a virtual network of customers, suppliers, and strategic alliances all working together and linked with high-octane IT systems that share information, which is open and immediate. Organisations that have highly effective networks do not leave them to chance. Such networks, both external and internal, are carefully designed, promoted and fostered.

Today's dynamic and global competitive environment creates continuous shifts in business strategy, potentially requiring associated shifts in organisation design. Key sources of competitive advantage and essential differences between corporate winners and losers will be the ability to respond to the pace of change; the capacity and speed of organisational learning; and the agility of the organisation to structure itself to best support the changing business strategies. More than ever, organisations that continue their legacy of bureaucratic, mechanistic structures and processes are less than effective. Organisations need structures that are flexible and adaptive. Managers need to understand not only basic organisation design concepts such as spans and layers but also need to understand the capacity of thoughtful organisation design to directly support business strategies and customer service. Structure follows strategy as form follows function.

There is no perfect organisation design. The design process requires the careful consideration of advantages and disadvantages of different options and making trade-offs. The process is about tailoring to the needs of the business. Equally, there is no perfect design process but what is clear is that the process starts with the strategy.

Finally, a word of warning: the structure of the organisation is not an end in itself. It is a very important piece in the jigsaw; an essential thread in the tapestry. However, other elements of organisational architecture such as strategy, systems and processes, effective people management, technology and metrics are equally important. Ultimate success comes from no one piece of the jigsaw but rather through careful design and integration of all the elements, not least of which is structure.

BIBLIOGRAPHY

Ackoff, R.L. (2006), *Idealised Design: How to Dissolve Tomorrow's Crisis...Today*, Pennsylvania: Wharton School Publishing.

Ackoff, R.L. (1994), *The Democratic Corporation: A Radical Perscription for Recreating Corporate America and Rediscovering Success*, New York: Oxford University Press.

Argyris, C. (1990), *Overcoming Organizational Defences: Facilitating Organizational Learning*, Englewood Cliffs, NJ: Prentice Hall.

Ashkenas, R., Ulrich, D., Jick, T. and Kerr, S. (2002), *The Boundaryless Organization: Breaking the Chains of Organisational Structure*, San Francisco: Jossey-Bass.

Austin, J. and Quinn, J. (2007), 'Ben & Jerry's: Preserving Mission and Brand within Unilever', Harvard Business School.

Bartlett, C., and Ghoshal, S. (1990), 'Matrix Management: Not a Structure, a Frame of Mind', *Harvard Business Review*, July – Aug.

Beckhard, R. and Harris, R., (1987), *Organizational Transitions: Managing Complex Change*, 2nd edition, Organisational Development series, US: Addison Wesley.

Beer, M., Eisenstat, R. and Spector, B. (1990), 'Why Change Programs Don't Produce Change', *Harvard Business Review*, Nov–Dec.

Bower, Joseph L. (2001), 'Not all M&As are Alike – and that Matters', *Harvard Business Review*, March.

Boxhall, P. and Purcell, J. (2003), *Strategy and Human Resource Management*, UK: Palgrave Macmillan.

Brett, J., Behfar, K. and Kern, M. (2006), 'Managing Multicultural Teams', *Harvard Business Review*, Nov.

Bridges, William (1991), *Managing Transitions*: *Making the Most of Change*, New York: Perseus Books.

Chandler, A. Jr. (1962), *Strategy and Structure*: *Chapters in the History of the American Industrial Enterprise*, Cambridge, MA: MIT Press.

Child, C. and Faulkner, D. (1998), 'Networks and Virtuality' in C. Child and D. Faulkner (eds.), *Strategies for Co-operation*: *Managing Alliances, Networks and Joint Ventures*, Oxford: Oxford University Press, 113–42.

Child, J. (2005), '*Organization*: *Contemporary Principles and Practices*, Oxford: Blackwell.

Cohen, S.G. (1993), 'New Approaches to Teams and Teamwork', in J.R. Galbraith, E.M. Lawler & Associates, *Organizing for the Future*: *The New Logic for Managing Complex Organizations*, US: Jossey-Bass, 194–225.

Collings, D.G, Morley, M.J. and Gunnigle, P. (2008), 'Composing the Top Management Team in the International Subsidiary: Qualitative Evidence on International Staffing in US MNCs in the Republic of Ireland', *Journal of World Business*, 43(2), in press.

Daft, R. (2001), *Organization Theory and Design*, 7th edition, Ohio: South-Western College Publishing.

Davis, M. and Weckler, D. (1996), *Organization Design*, California: Crisp Publications.

Epstein, Marc J. (2005), 'The Determinants and Evaluation of Merger Success', *Business Horizons* 48, Indiana University Kelley School of Business, 37–46.

Ettensen, R. and Knowles, J. (2006), 'Merging the Brands and Branding the Merger', *MIT Sloan Management Review*, Summer reprint no. 47410.

Fayol, H. (1949), *Industrial and General Administration*, London: Pitman & Sons.

Friedman, T. (2005), *The World is Flat*, New York: Picador.

Galbraith, J. (2002), *Designing Organisations*: *An Executive Briefing on Strategy, Structure and Process*, US: Jossey-Bass.

Grey, C. (2005), *A Very Short, Fairly Interesting and Reasonably Cheap Book about Studying Organizations,* Sage: London.

McShane, S.T. and Von Glinow, M.A (2003), *Organizational Behavior: Emerging Realities for the Workforce Revolution*, US: McGraw-Hill.

Merkle, J. (1980), *Management and Ideology,* Berkley: University of California Press.

Griffith, V. (1997), 'Teamwork's Own Goals', *Financial Times*, 18 July.

Handy, Charles (1995), *The Age of Unreason,* London: Arrow.

Harding, D. and Rouse, T. (2007), 'Human Due Diligence', *Harvard Business Review*, April.

Hecksher, C. (1994), 'Defining the Post-Bureaucratic Type', in C. Hecksher and A. Donnellan (eds.), *The Post-Bureaucratic Organization*: *New Perspectives on Organizational Change*, Thousand Oaks, CA: Sage.

Hellriegel, D., Slocum, J. and Woodman, R. (1998), *Organizational Behavior*, 8th edition, Ohio: South-Western College Publishing.

Herd, T., Saksena, A. and Steger, T. (2005), 'How Supply Chains Drive M&A Success', Harvard Business School Publishing, business newsletter.

Hofstede G. (1980), 'Motivation, Leadership and Organization: Do American Theories Apply Abroad?' *Organizational Dynamics*, 9, Summer, 42–63.

Howson, P. (2003), *Due Diligence*: *The Critical Stage in Mergers and Acquisitions*, Hampshire: Gower.

Huczynski, A. and Buchanan, D. (2001), *Organizational Behaviour*, 4th edition, UK: Prentice Hall.

Jick, T. (1995), *Managing Change*: *Cases and Concepts*, Irwin: McGraw Hill.

Katzenbach, J.R. and Smith, D.K. (1993), *The Wisdom of Teams: Creating the High Performance Organisation*, US: Harvard Business School Press.

Keats, B.W. and Hitt, M.A. (1988), 'A Causal Model of Linkages among Environmental Dimensions: Macro Organizational Characteristics', *Academy of Management Journal*, 31, 570–98.

Keats, B.W. and O'Neill, H.M. (2005), 'Organizational Structure: Looking through a Strategy Lens,' in M.A. Hitt, R.E. Freeman, and J. Harrison (eds.), *Handbook of Strategic Management* (2005), Oxford: Blackwell Publishing, 520–542.

Kotter, J. (1990), *A Force for Change: How Leadership Differs from Management*, US: The Free Press.

Lawler, E.E. III (1996), *From the Ground Up: Six Principles for Building the New Logic Corporation*, US: Jossey-Bass.

Mark, K. (2003), 'Deloitte and Touche: Integrating Arthur Anderson', Ref no. 9B04C004, Richard Ivey School of Business, University of Western Ontario.

Marks, M.L. and Mirvis, P.H. (1998), *Joining Forces: Making One Plus One Equal Three in Mergers, Acquisitions and Alliances*, US: Jossey Bass.

Mayer, D. (2004), Economic Action does not take place in a Vacuum', *Industry and Innovation*, Dec.

Miles, R., and Snow, C. (1978), *Organizational Strategy, Structure and Process*, New York: McGraw-Hill.

Mintzberg, H. (1990), 'The Design School: Reconsidering the Basic Premises of Strategic Management', *Strategic Management Journal*, 11,171–195.

Mintzberg, H. (1979), *The Structuring of Organizations*: *A Synthesis of Research*, Theory of Management Policy Series, NJ: Prentice-Hall.

Mintzberg, H. (1985), 'Of Strategies: Deliberate and Emergent', *Strategic Management Journal* 6, 257–272.

Mohrman, S.A. (1993), 'Integrating Roles and Structure in the Lateral Organisation' in Galbraith, J.R., Lawler, E.E. III, and associates (1993), *Organizing for the Future – The New Logic for Managing Complex Organizations*, US: Jossey-Bass, 109–141.

Morrison, A., Ricks, J., and Roth, K. (1991), 'Globalization versus Regionalization: Which Way for the Multinational?' *Organization Dynamics*, Winter, 17–29.

Nadler D., Gerstein, M., Shaw, R. and associates (1992), *Organizational Architecture – Designs for Changing Organizations*, US: Jossey Bass.

Nonaka, J. (2001), *Knowledge Emergence*: *Social, Technical and Evolutionary Dimensions of Knowledge Creation*, London: Oxford University Press.

Oliver Wyman Consultants: Delta Organization & Leadership, 'Strategic Organisation Design: an Integrated Approach', available at: <http://www.oliverwyman.com/ow/pdf_files/Strategic_Org Design_INS.pdf>, accessed January 2008.

Pettigrew, A. (1999), 'Organizing to Improve Company Performance', *Hot Topics*, 1(5), Warwick Business School, Warwick University.

Porter, M. (1980), *Competitive Strategy: Techniques for Analysing Industries and Competitors*, New York: Free Press.

Porter, M. (1987), 'From Competitive Advantage to Corporate Strategy', *Harvard Business Review*, May.

Prahalad, C.K. (2002), Foreword in R. Ashkenas, D. Ulrich, T. Jick and S. Kerr (eds.) (2002), *The Boundaryless Organization*, US: Jossey Bass.

Prashanth, K. (2004), 'Volvo's HR Practices: Focus on Job Enrichment', ICMR Case Catalogue, February 2005, available at: <http://icmr. icfai.org/PDF/Case_Catalog_February05.PDF>, accessed January 2008.

Procter & Gamble (2007), Annual Report, available at <http://www. pg.com/investors/annualreports.jhtml?_requestid=453411>, accessed February 2008.

Robbins, S. (1990), *Organization Theory*, US: Prentice-Hall.

Ruddock, A. (2007), *Michael O'Leary: A Life in Full Flight*, Dublin: Penguin Ireland.

Sorbonne University/Hay Management Consultants (2007), 'Dangerous Liaisons Report: Mergers and Acquisitions – The Integration Game', available at <http://www.peoplemanagement. co.uk>, accessed November 2007.

Taylor. F.W. (1911), *Principles of Scientific Management*, New York: Harper.

Tichey, N.M. (1983), *Managing Strategic Change: Technical, Political and Cultural Dynamics*, Wiley Series on Organizational Assessment and Change, US: John Wiley & Sons.

Trompenaars, F. and Hampden-Turner, C. (1998), *Riding the Waves of Culture: Understanding Diversity in Global Business,* New York: McGraw Hill.

Peters T.J. and Waterman R.H., (1982), *In Search of Excellence – Lessons from America's Best-Run Companies*, New York: Harper & Row.

Ulrich, D. (1997), *Human Resource Champions*, Harvard School Press.

Weber, J. (1996), 'The Upjohn-Pharmacia Merger', case 9-197-034, Harvard Business School.

Weber, M. (1947), *The Theory of Social and Economic Organization,* translated and edited by A. M. Henderson and T. Parsons, Oxford: Oxford University Press.

Wellins, R.S., Byham, W.C. and Wilson, J.M. (1993), *Empowered Teams*: *Creating Self-Directed Work Groups that Improve Quality, Productivity and Participation*, US: Jossey-Bass.

INDEX